How China S

Huiyun Feng • Kai He • Xiaojun Li

How China Sees the World

Insights From China's International Relations Scholars

Huiyun Feng
School of Government and
International Relations
Griffith University
Queensland, QLD, Australia

Kai He
Griffith Asia Institute
Griffith University
Queensland, QLD, Australia

Xiaojun Li
Department of Political Science
University of British Columbia
Vancouver, BC, Canada

ISBN 978-981-15-0481-5   ISBN 978-981-15-0482-2   (eBook)
https://doi.org/10.1007/978-981-15-0482-2

Cover illustration: © Patrick Foto / Getty Images

This Palgrave Macmillan imprint is published by the registered company Springer Nature
Singapore Pte Ltd.
The registered company address is: 152 Beach Road, #21-01/04 Gateway East, Singapore
189721, Singapore

ACKNOWLEDGMENTS

This is a small book on a big issue. China's rise generates unnerving questions: Are China and the United States doomed to fall into Thucydides's Trap? Is China going to challenge the world order? The mainstream international relations (IR) field is rife with discourses on potential conflict between China and the United States. However, do Chinese IR scholars see it the same way as Western scholars? How Chinese scholars see the world, China itself, and its relationship with the United States in the international system has significant implications for understanding China's rise and its ramifications for Asia and the world. Chinese scholars also tell Chinese IR stories in their own publications. Although it is still debatable to what extent Chinese scholars' views have an impact on Chinese decision making, it is undeniable that this group of political elites has significant influence on policy makers and Chinese society. This book is one of the first efforts to measure Chinese IR scholars' perceptions of key IR concepts and issues such as power, threats, relations between great powers, the international system, territorial conflict, and Chinese foreign policy.

This project would not have been possible without the generous support of the John D. and Catherine T. MacArthur Foundation (Grant No. 16-1512-150509-IPS). Kai He received an Australian Research Council Future Fellowship (Project ID: FT 160100355) in 2016, which also provided him precious time to work on this project in 2017–19. Griffith University has collaborated successfully with Tsinghua University's Institute of International Relations to conduct four years of opinion surveys in Beijing. We appreciate the institutional support from Griffith University and Tsinghua University. This project benefited tremendously from a large professional support team, who helped with carrying out surveys, collecting data, and organizing events. We are grateful to the Tsinghua team for their professional implementation of the surveys. We would also like to thank Stephen Walker, a mentor, friend, and advisor to this project, for his suggestions and advice. We thank our research assistants at Nankai University in China for diligently collecting the Chinese literature. We are grateful to Daniela Di Piramo and Dania Sheldon, who provided efficient and professional editorial assistance with this project. We would also like to thank Dr. John Fei and Dr. Angela Schlater, our grant officers at the MacArthur Foundation, for their support. Last but not least, we thank Vishal Daryanomel, our Palgrave Macmillan editor, for his encouragement and support.

Griffith University, Queensland, Australia   Huiyun Feng
Griffith University, Queensland, Australia   Kai He
University of British Columbia, Vancouver, Canada   Xiaojun Li

CONTENTS

ABOUT THE AUTHORS

Huiyun Feng is a senior lecturer in the School of Government and International Relations at Griffith University in Brisbane, Australia. She is a former Jennings Randolph Peace Scholar at the United States Institute of Peace. Her work has appeared in the *European Journal of International Relations, Security Studies, The Pacific Review, International Politics, Chinese Journal of International Politics,* and *Asian Perspective*. She is the author of *Chinese Strategic Culture and Foreign Policy Decision-Making: Confucianism, Leadership and War* (2007), the co-author of *Prospect Theory and Foreign Policy Analysis in the Asia Pacific: Rational Leaders and Risky Behavior* (2013), and the co-editor of *US–China Competition and the South China Sea Disputes* (2018), *Chinese Scholars and Foreign Policy: Debating International Relations* (2019), and *China's Challenges and International Order Transition: Beyond the "Thucydides Trap"* (2020).

Kai He is Professor of International Relations in the Griffith Asia Institute and Centre for Governance and Public Policy at Griffith University in Brisbane, Australia. He is an Australian Research Council Future Fellow (2017–2020) and a Visiting Chair Professor of International Relations at Nankai University, China (2018–2021). He was a post-doctoral fellow in the Princeton–Harvard China and the World Program (2009–2010). He is the author of *Institutional Balancing in the Asia Pacific: Economic Interdependence and China's Rise* (2009), the co-author of *Prospect Theory and Foreign Policy Analysis in the Asia Pacific: Rational Leaders and Risky Behavior* (2013), and the author of *China's Crisis Behavior: Political Survival and Foreign Policy* (2016).

Xiaojun Li is Assistant Professor of Political Science at the University of British Columbia in Vancouver, Canada. He has also held visiting positions at Harvard University's Fairbank Center for Chinese Studies (2014–2015), the Fudan Development Institute (2016), and the East–West Center (2018). His work has appeared in *Journal of Politics*, *International Studies Quarterly*, *Business and Politics*, *Canadian Journal of Political Science*, *Chinese Journal of International Politics*, *Foreign Policy Analysis*, *International Relations of the Asia-Pacific*, *Journal of Contemporary China*, *Journal of Experimental Political Science*, and *Pacific Affairs*, among others.

ACRONYMS

AIIB	Asian Infrastructure Investment Bank
ASEAN	Association of Southeast Asian Nations
BRI	Belt and Road Initiative
CCGA	Chicago Council on Global Affairs
CCPSIS	Chinese Community of Political Science and International Studies
CSIS	Center for Strategic and International Studies
EU	European Union
FONOPs	Freedom of Navigation Operations
IPE	international political economy
IR	international relations
MFN	most favored nation
NPT	Non-Proliferation Treaty
RCCC	Research Center for Contemporary China
SCO	Shanghai Cooperation Organization
UNSC	United Nations Security Council

LIST OF FIGURES

LIST OF TABLES

CHAPTER 1

Taking Chinese IR Scholars Seriously

China's rise is one of the defining episodes in twenty-first-century world politics. Scholars and pundits are fascinated by China's foreign policy behavior because what China does will shape the future of international politics. This is more important now than ever, as the escalating trade war between the United States and China might drag the whole world into a new Cold War. In order to explain and predict China's behavior, we need to know what Chinese leaders think about international relations (IR), because behavior is principally a function of perception.[1] Since it is difficult to gauge the mindsets of political leaders due to the political hierarchy and the complex nature of the decision-making process in state systems, scholars instead choose to examine public opinion to make sense of what leaders *should* think and perceive when facing constraints from society.

As this approach targets the public, it sometimes cannot explain the reality gap between public opinion and policy outcomes. For example, despite public fury over US behavior in the EP-3 mid-air collision incident on 1 April 2001, which saw the loss of a Chinese fighter jet and pilot, the Chinese government adopted an accommodative policy, releasing the US crew after the US ambassador to Beijing—instead of US officials from Washington DC—wrote a vaguely worded "sorry" letter several days after the incident.[2] This reality gap between public opinion and policy outcomes is not limited to authoritarian regimes such as China. In February 2003, Great Britain witnessed a very large public demonstration in opposition to

© The Author(s) 2019
H. Feng et al., *How China Sees the World*,
https://doi.org/10.1007/978-981-15-0482-2_1

the looming invasion of Iraq. But the expression of anti-war public opinion did not stop the Blair government from sending troops to Iraq.[3]

In this book, we intend to make sense of Chinese leaders' perceptions and attitudes about Chinese foreign policy through the eyes of China's international relations (IR) scholars. In doing so, we depart from most existing studies that survey the general public. Drawing on a unique, four-year opinion survey of Chinese IR scholars conducted at the annual conference of the Chinese Community of Political Science and International Studies (CCPSIS) in Beijing from 2014 to 2017, we empirically examine Chinese IR scholars' perceptions of and views on key issues related to China's international relations and how they change over time. In addition to this unique opinion survey method, we also rely on a traditional textual analysis approach to examine mainstream Chinese IR scholars' perceptions in China's top five IR journals. Through comparing and contrasting our opinion surveys and textual analyses of published journal articles, we can more confidently and precisely measure how Chinese IR scholars view the world and China's position in it.

It should be emphasized that we do not claim Chinese IR scholars' views necessarily represent or influence the perceptions of Chinese leaders or the Chinese government. Nor are we trying to demonstrate *how* Chinese IR scholars can influence Chinese leaders' decisions in foreign policy. Instead, we focus on examining *what* Chinese IR scholars think and perceive in the domain of China's foreign policy and international relations. Nevertheless, this should be important in and of itself. As Daniel Lynch points out, "studying these [Chinese scholars'] images can be useful in trying to assess what trajectory [Chinese foreign policy] is likely to become, precisely because the elites are operating inside parameters imposed by the (still) awesomely powerful Party-state."[4] By revealing not merely the "public opinions" but the "policy opinions" of Chinese IR scholars regarding key issues related to Chinese foreign policy, we hope to provide some approximation of Chinese leaders' mindsets on international relations and therefore set a foundation for future research on the impacts of Chinese IR scholars on foreign policy.

There are three sections in this introductory chapter. First, we discuss the existing research on China's public opinion and foreign policy and suggest that the general, public-targeted survey research faces three analytical weaknesses. Second, we introduce our unique "opinion survey and textual analysis" approach, which integrates survey research techniques and traditional textual analyses of Chinese IR scholars' writings. Third, we introduce the structure of the book and lay out the major findings.

PUBLIC OPINION RESEARCH ON CHINESE FOREIGN POLICY[5]

In the study of Chinese foreign policy, the role of public opinion has long been neglected.[6] This is somewhat understandable, as China is a one-party state and the foreign-policy decision-making process remains relatively confidential and inaccessible to the general public and the outside world. However, with widespread Internet use and commercialized media, the Chinese government faces increasing public scrutiny of its foreign-policy decisions. The growing importance of public opinion in Chinese foreign policy making requires scholars from China and abroad to more systematically study the Chinese public's opinions on foreign policy issues.

Following Gabriel Almond's 1950 classic work, *The American People and Foreign Policy*, we differentiate three strata of the Chinese populace.[7] Previous studies show that there are normally three types of publics in society: policy elites, sub-elites, and the masses. Policy elites include leaders and key decision makers in government. The masses refer to the (uninformed) general public. The sub-elite group comprises the informed public, including scholars, analysts, and members of the media who work on international affairs; it is located in between the policy elite and the general public. As mentioned earlier, due to the difficulties of accessing the mindsets of policy makers, most existing research focuses on examining opinion at the general public level and can be grouped into four types.

First, there exists some indigenous polling/survey research conducted by major Chinese newspapers. In 1993, the *China Youth Daily*, the Communist Youth League of China's official newspaper, established a Public Survey Center. Over the years, this center has conducted several public polls on the attitudes of Chinese youth toward the West. In May 1995, after the United States bombed the Chinese embassy in Belgrade, the center published a survey report entitled "Chinese Youth Sees the World," which showed that the United States was the most disliked country among Chinese youth. The center later claimed that this survey result "influenced Clinton's policy toward China."[8] In addition, some other leading IR-focused newspapers, such as *The Global Times*—which is affiliated with the official party newspaper, the *People's Daily*—also periodically conduct online or newspaper-based public opinion polls regarding China's foreign relations.

It is difficult to evaluate how representative and reliable these polling results are, since the methodologies and survey techniques are never published, making it impossible to assess the validity of the results against social scientific criteria.[9] It is also difficult to evaluate whether and to what extent the government played a role in implementing these surveys to serve its own interests, given the hierarchical relationship between the party and these official newspapers. In addition to media outlets, some Chinese research institutions, such as the Chinese Academy of Social Sciences, also periodically conduct public opinion surveys.[10] Given these Chinese research institutions' official background and consequent lack of independence, the reliability of their survey results is subject to a similar critique as Chinese newspapers.

Second, some international research institutions have also conducted public opinion surveys in China, often as part of a larger multi-country study. For example, the Chicago Council on Global Affairs (CCGA) has directed large-scale public opinion surveys around the world, including in China. In 2007, the CCGA and WorldPublicOpinion.org collaborated with organizations in other countries for a public opinion survey on the rises of China and India. In 2008, the CCGA conducted a six-nation public opinion survey examining the current and potential use of soft power in East Asia.[11] In 2001, the Pew Research Center launched its "Pew Global Attitudes Project," and China was an important part of the initial survey. In October 2012, the project released its latest in-depth analysis of Chinese public opinion about a range of issues, from satisfaction with family life to attitudes toward the United States.[12]

The public online surveys conducted by international research institutions and think tanks are, in general, better designed and employ random sampling.[13] With sample sizes ranging from 1000 to 3000, these surveys can more accurately grasp "true" public attitudes on issues related to IR. For example, the Pew Global Attitudes Project reported that a third of the respondents in 2008 viewed the United States as an enemy of China.[14] In a 2009 survey by the Lowy Institute for International Policy, about 45% of the participants opined that the United States posed the greatest or second-greatest threat to China's security.[15] In both surveys, Japan was seen as the next greatest threat.

The third type of studies has been conducted by US-trained IR scholars, often in collaboration with major Chinese universities. One of the early pioneers is Chen Jie, a political scientist from the United States, who conducted a public opinion survey with the People's University in Beijing in 1999. The survey randomly sampled 720 Beijing residents' perceptions regarding military threats to China. Their final report showed that a majority of respondents (75%) agreed that the United States intended to threaten China.[16] Another notable collaborative research project was a survey conducted by Zhejiang University and Valparaiso University in 2001. The random sample for this survey was 750 well-educated people from non-Beijing areas. They were asked about their attitudes toward the United States and America's China policy. The results of this survey indicated that only 12% of the respondents saw America as China's major enemy, although 49% regarded US–China relations as unfriendly.[17] In a more recent study, a team of researchers sampled 2579 households in four Chinese municipalities through the Research Center for Contemporary China (RCCC) to explore Chinese urban residents' attitudes toward Japan and South Korea in 2010.[18] They found that generalized trust, or the belief that other nations have benign intentions, was the most important driving force behind respondents' trust of Japan and South Korea. This sort of trust has a positive effect on preferences for interstate cooperation.

The last type of studies involves surveys conducted with Chinese netizens. This method of participant recruitment has become increasingly popular, thanks to the emergence of commercial marketing research firms such as SoJump, Diaoyan Bao, Qualtrics, and Survey Sampling International, as well as online crowdsourcing platforms such as Zhubajie.[19] These firms, either on their own or through local Chinese affiliates, maintain large online panels of potential survey participants. Recent studies using online surveys of netizens have explored a wide range of foreign policy topics, including public attitudes toward international leadership, preferences for the resolution of territorial disputes, support for foreign direct investment, peacekeeping operations, and the use of force.[20] The flexibility of online surveys has also made it possible for researchers to implement more sophisticated designs. A number of recent studies, for example, have used online survey experiments to examine the sources and consequences of domestic audience cost in China.[21]

While studies of general public opinion on foreign policy in China have made significant inroads and produced important findings, there are three analytical problems. First, it is still debatable whether the general public has a stable, coherent, and informed opinion. Among American public opinion scholars, this question has driven the debate between the Almond–Lippmann Consensus and its challengers since the 1970s.[22] The fact that similar survey questions can yield different responses with different samples at different time periods is evident in the large discrepancies between the results of the two surveys cited above on China's public attitude toward America.

Assessing whether and how public opinion shifts over time requires longitudinal surveys, but these are often difficult to implement due to various constraints. One exception is the Beijing Area Study (BAS), led by Alastair Iain Johnston and implemented by the RCCC.[23] Analyzing the 1998–2004 annual survey data of the BAS implemented by the RCCC, Johnston showed that China's middle class exhibited "a greater level of nascent liberalism than poorer income groups," and Beijing's middle class surprisingly held a relatively high level of amity toward the United States.[24] Nevertheless, the BAS is restricted to one city, and the results may not represent the views of the public in other parts of China. Johnston concludes that China's public opinion is diverse at the societal level, and that it is difficult to achieve a generalizable or constant measurement of public opinion in China.

Second, public opinion surveys measure respondents' stated preferences, so they are subject to social desirability bias, satisficing, and other cognitive biases common to self-reported responses in survey research.[25] These biases are even more serious in China, where people may have a bigger incentive to hide their true opinion and give answers that conform to social norms, especially when it comes to sensitive foreign policy issues. As one leading Chinese IR scholar, Wang Jisi, points out:

> [T]here is a phenomenon called "silent majority" in the Chinese society. It means that the majority in the Chinese public does not like to express their opinions and views publicly, especially on the Internet. Therefore, some extreme views appeared to dominate the public discourse in China which leads to some misunderstanding between the true public opinion and these extreme views in the society.[26]

Although these two problems challenge the internal and external validity of public opinion surveys, they can be remedied by carefully designed sampling procedures, longitudinal surveys, and item count techniques (such as list experiments). But the third analytical problem, namely the causal linkage between public opinion and foreign policy, is the most challenging one. Generally speaking, it is still unclear whether leaders' decisions are influenced by public opinion or public opinion is manipulated by leaders. Although the pluralist theory of democracy assumes that the general public has a significant impact on the foreign policy decision-making process, Winston Churchill reminded us that there is "no such thing as public opinion. There is only published opinion."[27] Scholarly works also question the causal link between public opinion and foreign policy, warning that the general public may not have enough knowledge about foreign policy issues, or they may not even care about foreign policy in comparison with domestic issues.[28]

The causal linkage between public opinion and foreign policy is even more problematic in authoritarian regimes such as China. On the one hand, given the nature of the Chinese political system, the public may not have the appropriate channels to transmit their attitudes on foreign policy issues to the government. On the other hand, since authoritarian leaders do not face the same electoral pressure as their democratic counterparts, they do not need to maintain a high level of responsiveness to the public. This has led some scholars to suggest that in China, so-called public opinion is actually a result and not a source of governmental policy.[29] Other scholars further point out that Chinese foreign policy decision making is widely seen as the elite's business, while general public opinion stays far away from the decision-making process.[30]

READING CHINESE IR SCHOLARS: AN "OPINION SURVEY AND TEXTUAL ANALYSIS" APPROACH

The above discussions suggest that in evaluating the connection between public opinion and China's foreign policy, what is important is not to measure all types of public opinion but to understand which opinion group matters the most in social and political discourses. We argue that one such group is Chinese IR scholars. As many China watchers have argued, Chinese IR scholars can serve as mediators between the Chinese leadership and the general public.[31] They have better access to foreign policy decision makers in the government and thus are able to provide policy consultations and recommendations. They also write academic papers, publish editorials and blog opinion pieces, and conduct TV interviews to educate the mass public on a wide range of issues, from US–China relations to the North Korean nuclear crisis.

Furthermore, the views of Chinese IR scholars can open a unique and rare window into understanding China's foreign policies and international relations. There is an increasing research trend to use elite views to make sense of IR.[32] Given the difficulty of gaining access to the top elites in China, however, sub-elites such as scholars are the second-best option. By measuring how these IR scholars perceive Chinese power capabilities, bilateral relations, and broader foreign policy goals, we may be able to infer how China's policy makers might view various IR issues.

It should be acknowledged that scholars have long tried to study Chinese foreign policy and US–China relations through Chinese IR scholars. In his ground-breaking 1991 book *Beautiful Imperialist*, David Shambaugh examined the conceptual lenses through which the so-called America watchers[33] in China perceived the United States between 1972 and 1990, suggesting that China's distorted and biased perceptions of the United States contributed to the fluctuations in US–China relations during the Cold War.[34] After the Cold War, many scholars have followed Shambaugh's footsteps, monitoring China's changing perceptions of the United States.[35] For example, Philip Saunders examines how China's America watchers perceived the United States in the 1990s and suggests that Chinese analysts and scholars have improved their understanding of the United States, but the quality and knowledge level of the broader community of America watchers still vary widely.[36]

Traditionally, most research on America watchers in particular or Chinese IR scholars in general relies on either analyses of their written works or one-on-one interviews. Although these studies have yielded insightful findings, three potential problems exist. First, due to the party's censorship of written publications, Chinese America watchers may not be able to publish written works that reflect their true perceptions. For example, China's *Southern Weekend* was forced to change their editorial statement on New Year's Eve of 2013 because the original version contained sensitive phrases such as "constitutional reform."[37] Although scholarly work might be subject to less restrictive monitoring, scholars may exercise "self-censorship" to avoid jeopardizing their professional careers.[38]

A second potential problem is that one-on-one interviews pose similar dilemmas as written publications. During interviews with foreign scholars, Chinese scholars may not want to reveal views and perceptions that stray far from the party line. While most existing research utilizes anonymity to protect interviewees' identities, scholars retain legitimate conscious or subconscious concern about the consequences of what they say during interviews.

Finally, both textual analysis and interviews have the potential for subjective or sampling bias in their research design. Although no social science research can claim perfect objectivity, textual analysis and interviews rely particularly heavily on researchers' subjective interpretations of written materials or oral exchanges with interviewees. In addition, which written texts are selected and which interviewees are available are sometimes beyond researchers' control. The result may be a biased sample that could undermine the quality of the research.

In this book, we adopt an analytical framework that combines the strengths of both public opinion surveys and textual analysis to examine Chinese IR scholars' perceptions of international relations. The first part of our "opinion survey and textual analysis" is based on a series of surveys we conducted at the annual conference of CCPSIS between 2014 and 2017. The CCPSIS was founded by Tsinghua University's Institute of International Relations in the winter of 2008, and it has held its annual conference every July in Beijing since 2009. Over the past decade, the CCPSIS annual conference has become the largest and most influential academic meeting in China's IR circle. In 2015, the two-day conference attracted 116 themed panels, over 400 panelists, and 961 recorded attendees from major universities and think tanks across China.[39] In other words, while CCPSIS participants may not constitute a representative sample of Chinese IR scholars throughout the country, they are as close as one can get.

Only one previous study has attempted to study sub-elite opinions on foreign policy issues in China: the "US–China Security Perceptions Project" launched by the Pew Research Center Global Attitudes Project in 2012 in collaboration with the Carnegie Endowment of International Peace, the Kissinger Institute on China and the United States at the Woodrow Wilson International Center for Scholars, the China Strategic Culture Promotion Association, and the Research Center for Contemporary China at Peking University. This project evaluated the different views of the general public and experts in both the United States and China regarding US–China security issues. The Chinese portion of the project surveyed 358 individuals, comprised of 75 government officials, 149 scholars at military and non-military research institutes, 70 business and trade leaders, and 64 media professionals.[40]

Our survey shares the Pew project's premise: we believe that China's IR scholars play a distinct role in influencing China's foreign policy, although identifying the causal mechanism is beyond the scope of this research. Unlike the Pew project, which was conducted once, we were able to implement the survey for a four-year period, a rare feat that is unlikely to be repeated in the foreseeable future, given the tightened political atmosphere in China since the 19th Party Congress in October 2017.[41]

We used a similar questionnaire at the CCPSIS conferences for the four years, although we made minor updates to some questions to reflect new developments or events impacting China's foreign policy. The questionnaire contains about 50 multiple-choice questions and is organized around three main issue areas (for details about our questionnaire, please see the Appendix):

- perceptions of China's own power (hard military, economic, political, comprehensive power, and soft cultural power), especially in comparison with the United States, in the international system
- perceptions of China's foreign relations with other major powers (the United States, Japan, Russia, Africa, Latin America, the Association of Southeast Asian Nations (ASEAN), India, and Europe)
- perceptions of China's key foreign policies (e.g., the keep-a-low-profile principle; the non-alliance policy; and North Korea's nuclear proliferation issue)

We distributed the questionnaires at the conference registration table and collected them with the assistance of the conference staff from Tsinghua University in Beijing. The questionnaire was accessible to all participants at the conference, and completion was entirely voluntary. We did not record any personal information to ensure that participants could answer the questions truthfully without having to worry about their responses being linked to their identities. The total number of conference participants every year is around 800. We collected and recorded a total of 1251 completed questionnaires, with a response rate of around 30–40% through the four years.

Table 1.1 summarizes the profiles of the survey participants in 2014–2017. Overall, the vast majority are Chinese citizens (97%). Nearly 60% are males. About half are students (including PhD students), and a little over a quarter are university professors and researchers.[42] Over 80% are between 20 and 40 years old. More than one-third hold a master's or doctoral degree, and more than two-thirds have overseas experience. These statistics suggest that our survey sample represents a distinct group of people: highly educated IR scholars or future IR scholars in Chinese society.

Looking across the four survey years, we can see that over time, many of the demographics of the participants do not vary much over time—age,

Table 1.1 Profiles of participants in the CCPSIS surveys (2014–2017)

Variable	2014	2015	2016	2017	p-value	Overall
Male	60.23	63.66	63.52	54.46	0.03	60.56
Age						
<20	2.29	3.17	3.44	6.98	0.02	4.02
20–30	60.31	59.65	53.75	54.92	0.25	57.07
30–40	25.95	27.09	27.50	21.90	0.35	25.64
40–50	9.54	8.07	11.25	13.65	0.12	10.61
50–60	1.15	1.73	2.50	1.59	0.65	1.77
>60	0.76	0.29	1.25	0.63	0.53	0.88
Occupation						
Students	48.86	49.14	46.88	56.19	0.10	50.28
University prof/researcher	31.44	29.02	25.94	26.03	0.39	27.99
Think tank researcher	6.44	9.48	11.56	11.43	0.14	9.86
Journalists	5.30	2.59	4.38	2.86	0.24	3.69
Government officials	4.17	1.72	0.63	1.27	0.01	1.84
Freelancers	1.89	3.16	5.94	0.95	0.00	3.05
Others	1.89	4.89	4.69	1.27	0.02	3.29
Overseas experience	60.23	60.81	56.29	59.62	0.65	59.23
Education						
BA/BS	26.52	23.28	19.18	28.34	0.04	24.20
MA/MS	44.70	41.38	44.65	35.99	0.10	41.56
PhD	28.79	35.34	36.16	35.67	0.21	34.24
Last year attendance	n.a.	66.57	62.78	74.43	0.01	67.80
Chinese nationality	99.23	98.20	96.21	95.82	0.03	97.38
Sample size	264	350	320	317		1251

gender (more balanced in 2017), education, and occupation. Furthermore, the majority of our respondents reported having attended the conferences in previous years. While we cannot control and trace the respondents as in a real longitudinal survey, these comparisons suggest that the annual meeting setting of the CCPSIS makes the respondents (Chinese IR scholars) comparable across different years. This allows us to construct a semi-longitudinal dataset that can then be used to capture the changing attitudes and perceptions of Chinese IR scholars.

In the second part of our "opinion survey and textual analysis," we use traditional textual analysis of published IR scholarship to complement the survey findings. Here, we collected articles from five top Chinese IR journals and analyzed the main topics and trends in those articles in relation to our survey questions. The five IR journals are: *Journal of Contemporary Asia-Pacific Studies* (当代亚太), *World Economics and*

Politics (世界经济与政治), *Contemporary International Relations* (现代国际关系), *Foreign Affairs Review* (外交评论), and *China International Studies* (国际问题研究). *Journal of Contemporary Asia-Pacific Studies* and *World Economy and Politics* are affiliated with the Chinese Academy of Social Sciences. The third is an official journal of the China Institute of Contemporary International Relations, a leading policy think tank in China. *Foreign Affairs Review* is run by China Foreign Affairs University and *China International Studies* by the China Institute of International Studies, and both have close affiliations with the Chinese Foreign Ministry. Due to the relatively slow process and possible lag effect of printed publications, we extended the timeframe of our publication collection by one year on both ends so that we could be more confident in comparing and contrasting our textual analysis results from printed publications with our survey findings. The total number of scholarly publications in our textual analysis is 434 (90 in 2013, 69 in 2014, 77 in 2015, 73 in 2016, 74 in 2017, and 51 in 2018).

STRUCTURE OF THE BOOK

The rest of the book is divided according to the three issue areas in our survey. Chapter 2 discusses how Chinese IR scholars view the structure of the international system, China's position in the international system, and China's power capabilities in various dimensions (economic, military, etc.) in comparison with those of the United States. It also traces the changing perceptions of Chinese IR scholars in our survey from 2014 to 2017 regarding the potential power transition between the United States and China. We then compare the survey findings with our textual analysis of scholarly publications on China's power capabilities and the international order transition. One major finding is that Chinese IR scholars are very confident about China's rising capabilities, especially its economic power, but they do not think China will replace the US hegemony in the foreseeable future. In other words, in the eyes of Chinese IR scholars, there is no causal linkage between China's rise and America's decline. Furthermore, they do not see China as a challenger to the current international order.

Chapter 3 examines how Chinese IR scholars view US–China relations in both the short and the long run. We asked respondents how they would describe both the current status of the relationship and its future trajectory. In particular, this chapter focuses on how Chinese IR scholars perceived

1 TAKING CHINESE IR SCHOLARS SERIOUSLY   13

the challenges and problems as well as common interests and opportunities in current and future US–China relations. Our textual analyses of scholarly publications also examine these same issues in the US–China bilateral relationship. Through comparing our opinion survey results and textual analysis findings, we suggest that the views of Chinese IR scholars are pragmatic and consistent regarding both problems and opportunities in US–China relations. They highlighted the influence of security-related matters, such as the Taiwan Strait issue and the South China Sea disputes, over US–China relations. However, they did not expect that the bilateral trade imbalance and economic friction could trigger a "trade war" between the United States and China in 2017, which likely took a lot of people by surprise.

Chapter 4 examines how Chinese IR scholars view China's foreign relations with other major powers and players in world politics, including Japan, Russia, India, the Association of Southeast Asian Nations, the European Union, African nations, and Latin American countries. In addition, this chapter explores how Chinese IR scholars view China's own foreign policies, such as the non-alliance principle and Deng Xiaoping's keeping-a-low-profile doctrine. It also examines how Chinese IR scholars changed or retained their perceptions of China's foreign policies over the four-year period from 2014 to 2017. Once again, we compare and contrast our textual analyses of scholarly publications with the opinion survey findings. The results show that Chinese IR scholars have a disquieting view of Japan's possible conflicts with China in the East China Sea. In contrast, China's relations with Russia are positively perceived, but Chinese IR scholars in their publications also highlight that economic cooperation is the weakest link between the two nations. One interesting finding on Chinese foreign policy is the discrepancy between our opinion surveys and textual analyses. For example, although our surveys show that most scholars support a change in foreign policy toward North Korea, Chinese scholarly publications do not convey the same message. Similarly, respondents to our surveys support a change in China's "keeping-a-low-profile" policy principle, but few Chinese publications deliver the same argument, likely because China has not yet officially abandoned the principle. This discrepancy shows that Chinese scholars are still hesitant to challenge official policies in their publications.

The concluding chapter discusses what we have learned from our research on Chinese IR scholars through our unique "opinion survey and textual analysis" approach, as well as the implications of the findings for our understanding of China's rise. We further examine China's security concerns and related perceptions of future conflicts. Then we go beyond our survey and textual analyses to share our concluding thoughts on the future of US–China relations. We argue that the United States and China need to cooperate if they are to share leadership and prestige as well as cope with common challenges in the future.

This book makes two contributions to the study of China's international relations. On the one hand, we fill an intellectual gap in the study of Chinese IR scholars' perceptions of international relations in the 2010s. Through a unique analytical approach integrating opinion surveys and textual analysis, our research paves a new way for studying Chinese public opinion and China's foreign policy. On the other hand, through the eyes of Chinese IR scholars, we make sense of what Chinese policy makers may think about the world. If augmenting mutual understanding is the first step to forging a peaceful relationship between the United States and China in the twenty-first century, this book will open a unique window for China watchers and policy makers to comprehend how China thinks and what China wants. China's rise can be peaceful, but China cannot achieve this on its own.

NOTES

1. David Shambaugh, *Beautiful Imperialist: China Perceives America, 1972–1990* (Princeton: Princeton University Press, 1991), 3.
2. Michael Swaine and Zhang Tuosheng, eds. *Managing Sino-American Crises: Case Studies and Analysis* (Washington D.C.: Carnegie Endowment for International Peace, 2006); Edward Slingerland, Eric Blanchard, and Lyn Boyd-Judson, "Collision with China: Conceptual Metaphor Analysis, Somatic Marking, and the EP-3 Incident," *International Studies Quarterly* 51(2007): 53–77; and Wu Xinbo, "Understanding Chinese and U.S. Crisis Behavior," *The Washington Quarterly* 31, no. 1 (2008): 61–76.
3. BBC News, "Million March against Iraq War," 16 February 2003, available at: www.bbcnews.co.uk.
4. Daniel Lynch, *China's Futures: PRC Elites Debate Economics, Politics, and Foreign Policy* (Stanford: Stanford University Press, 2015), x.
5. This section is based on the following two publications: Huiyun Feng and Kai He, "America in the Eyes of America Watchers: Survey Research in Beijing in 2012," *The Journal of Contemporary China* 24, no. 91 (2015): 83–100; Huiyun Feng and Kai He, "How Chinese Scholars Think about Chinese Foreign Policy," *Australian Journal of Political Science* 51, no. 4 (2016): 694–710.

6. It is worth noting that the majority of public opinion surveys conducted in China focus on topics in comparative politics such as economic change, political development, and ethnic issues rather than foreign policy issues. See, for example, Yanlai Wang, Nicholas Rees, and Bernadette Andreosso-O'Callaghan, "Economic Change and Political Development in China: Findings from a Public Opinion Survey," *Journal of Contemporary China* 13, no. 39 (2004): 203–222; Chack-kie Wong and Peter Nana-Shong Lee, "Economic Reform and Social Welfare: The Chinese Perspective Portrayed through a Social Survey in Shanghai," *Journal of Contemporary China* 10, no. 28 (2001): 517–532. On ethnic relations, see Herbert S. Yee "Ethnic Relations in Xinjiang: A Survey of Uygur-Han relations in Urumqi," *Journal of Contemporary China* 12, no. 35 (2003): 431–452; Wenfang Tang and Benjamin Darr, "Chinese Nationalism and its Political and Social Origins," *Journal of Contemporary China* 21, no. 77 (2012): 811–826; Jie Chen, "Sociopolitical Attitudes of the Masses and Leaders in the Chinese Village: Attitude Congruence and Constraint," *Journal of Contemporary China* 14, no. 44 (2005): 445–464; Zhengxu Wang "Public Support for Democracy in China," *Journal of Contemporary China* 16, no. 53 (2007): 561–579; David V. Dowd, Allen Carlson, and Shen Mingming, "The Prospects for Democratization in China: Evidence from the 1995 Beijing Area Study," *Journal of Contemporary China* 8, no. 22 (1999): 365–380. For a comprehensive review of survey research in Chinese politics, see Melanie Manion, "A survey of survey research on Chinese politics: what have we learned?" *Contemporary Chinese Politics: New Sources, Methods, and Field Strategies* (Cambridge, UK: Cambridge University Press, 2010), 181–199; Xiaojun Li, "New Trends in Survey Research on Chinese Politics," Memo for the Harvard Chinese Politics Workshop (2018), http://cnpoliticsworkinggroup.org/wp-content/uploads/2018/02/Xiaojun-Li_Survey-Research.pdf.

7. Gabriel Almond, *The American People and Foreign Policy* (New York: Harcourt, 1950).

8. See the official website of the Public Survey Center, available at: http://www.minyi.net.cn/minyi_about.php.

9. For a similar criticism, see Melanie Manion, "A Survey of Survey Research on Chinese Politics," in Allen Carlson, Mary Gallagher, Kenneth Lieberthal, and Melanie Manion, eds. *Contemporary Chinese Politics: New Sources, Methods, and Field Strategies* (Cambridge: Cambridge University Press, 2010), 181–199.

10. Li Shenming, ed. *Zhengguo Minzhong de Guojiguan* [Chinese Public View of the World] (Beijing: Social Sciences Academic Press, 2012).

11. See the Chicago Council on Global Affairs website, available at: http://www.thechicagocouncil.org/pos_overview.php. Some scholars have used

the CCGA data to conduct research on China. See Tao Xie and Benjamin I. Page, "Americans and the Rise of China as a World Power," *Journal of Contemporary China* 19, no. 65 (2010): 479–501.

12. See The Pew Global Attitudes Project Website, available at: http://pew-global.org. For a China-related study using the Pew Global Attitudes project data, see Tao Xie and Benjamin I. Page, "What Affects China's National Image? A Cross-National Study of Public Opinion,' *Journal of Contemporary China* 22, no. 83 (2013): 850–867.

13. It is difficult to follow a random sampling strategy in China since the samples are normally drawn disproportionately from urban areas.

14. Available at: www.pewglobal.org.

15. Fergus Hanson and Andrew Shearer, *China and the World: Public opinion and Foreign policy* (Sydney: Lowy Institute for International Policy, 2009).

16. Jie Chen, "Urban Chinese Perceptions of Threats from the United States and Japan," *Public Opinion Quarterly* 65, no. 2 (2001): 254–266.

17. Yu Sunda et al., "Sino-U.S. Relations: Views from the Masses," *World Economics and Politics*, no. 6 (2001): 33–38. 余逊达、陈旭东、朱纪平，"中美关系: 来自民众的看法", 世界经济与政治, 第六期, 2001 年, 33–38 页.

18. Xiaojun Li, Jianwei Wang, and Dingding Chen. "Chinese Citizens' Trust in Japan and South Korea: Findings from a Four-City Survey." *International Studies Quarterly* 60, no. 4 (2016): 778–789.

19. Xiaojun Li, Weiyi Shi, and Boliang Zhu. "The face of internet recruitment: Evaluating the labor markets of online crowdsourcing platforms in China." *Research & Politics* 5, no. 1 (2018): 1–8.

20. Burzo, Stefano, and Xiaojun Li. "Public Perceptions of International Leadership in China and the United States." *Chinese Political Science Review* 3, no. 1 (2018): 81–99. Xiaojun Li and Ka Zeng. "Individual preferences for FDI in developing countries: Experimental evidence from China." *Journal of Experimental Political Science* 4, no. 3 (2017): 195–205; Songying Fang and Xiaojun Li. "Historical Ownership and Territorial Disputes," *Journal of Politics* (forthcoming); Songying Fang and Fanglu Sun. "Gauging Chinese Public Support for China's Role in Peacekeeping." *The Chinese Journal of International Politics* 12, no. 2 (2019): 179–201; Jessica Chen Weiss, "How Hawkish Is the Chinese Public? Another Look at "Rising Nationalism" and Chinese Foreign Policy", *Journal of Contemporary China* 28, no. 119 (2019): 679–695.

21. Kai Quek and Alastair Iain Johnston. "Can China Back Down? Crisis De-escalation in the Shadow of Popular Opposition." *International Security* 42, no. 3 (2018): 7–36; Mark S. Bell and Kai Quek. "Authoritarian Public Opinion and the Democratic Peace." *International Organization* 72, no. 1 (2018): 227–242; Jessica Chen Weiss and Allan Dafoe.

"Authoritarian audiences and government rhetoric in international crises: Evidence from China." *International Studies Quarterly* (2019) https:// doi.org/10.1093/isq/sqz059. Xiaojun Li and Dingding Chen, "Public Opinion, International Reputation, and Audience Cost in an Authoritarian Regime," University of British Columbia.

22. Ole R. Holsti, "Public Opinion and Foreign Policy: Challenges to the Almond-Lippmann Consensus," *International Studies Quarterly* 36 (1992): 439–466; Holsti, *Public Opinion and American Foreign Policy*, revised edition (Ann Arbor: The University of Michigan Press, 2004); and Robert Y. Shapiro and Benjamin I. Page, "Foreign Policy and the Rational Public," *The Journal of Conflict Resolution* 32, no. 2 (1988): 211–247.

23. Alastair Iain Johnston, "The Correlates of Beijing Public Opinion toward the United States, 1998–2004," in Alastair Iain Johnston and Robert Ross, eds. *New Directions in the Study of China's Foreign Policy* (Stanford: Stanford University Press, 2006), 340–379.

24. Alastair Iain Johnston, "Chinese Middle Class Attitudes Towards: International Affairs: Nascent Liberalization?" *The China Quarterly* 179 (2004): 603–628.

25. Norbert Schwarz, "Self-reports: how the questions shape the answers". *American Psychologist* 54, no. 2 (1999), 93; Jon Kronick, Charles Judd, and Bernd Wittenbrink, "The Measurement of Attitudes." In Dolores Albarracín, Blair T. Johnson, and Mark P. Zanna (eds.) *The Handbook of Attitudes* (New York, NY: Psychology Press, 2005): 21–76.

26. Wang Jisi and Susan Shirk, "Dialogue: Public Opinion and Foreign Policy," *Global Times*, 16 January 2004, Section 15.

27. For the pluralist view of democracy and public opinion, see Benjamin Page and Robert Shapiro, "Effects of Public Opinion on Policy," *American Political Science Review* 77, no. 1 (1983): 175–190. For competing arguments, see Noam Chomsky and Edward Herman, *Manufacturing Consent* (New York: Pantheon, 1988) and Michael Margolis and Gary Mauser, eds. *Manipulating Public Opinion: Essays on Public Opinion as a Dependent Variable* (Belmont: Wadsworth, 1989).

28. James Rosenau, *Public Opinion and Foreign Policy* (New York: Random House, 1961); Benjamin Ginsberg, *The Captive Public: How Mass Opinion Promotes State Power* (New York: Basic Books, 1986).

29. Yun Sun, "Chinese Public Opinion: Shaping China's Foreign Policy, or Shaped by It?" December 2011, available at: http://www.brookings.edu/ research/opinions/2011/12/13-china-public-opinion-sun; and Linda Jakobson and Dean Knox, "New Foreign Policy Actors in China," SIPRI Policy Paper, 26 September 2010.

30. Joseph Fewsmith and Stanley Rosen, "The Domestic Context of Chinese Foreign Policy: Does 'Public Opinion' Matter?" in David Lampton, ed.

The Making of Chinese Foreign and Security Policy in the Era of Reform, 1978–2000 (Stanford: Stanford University Press, 2001), 151–190, at 152.

31. Shambaugh, *Beautiful Imperialist*; Philip Saunders, "China's America Watchers: Changing Attitudes toward the U.S.," *The China Quarterly* 161, (2000): 41–65.

32. Michael Tomz, Jessica Weiss, and Keren Yarhi-Milo, "Public Opinion and Decisions about Military Force in Democracies," *International Organization, forthcoming.*

33. China's "America watchers" refers to Chinese academic scholars and policy analysts who study US–China relations in government-funded universities and research institutions.

34. Shambaugh, *Beautiful Imperialist.*

35. Jianwei Wang, *Limited Adversaries, Sino-American Mutual Images in the Post-Cold War Era* (Oxford: Oxford University Press, 2000); Biwu Zhang, "Chinese Perceptions of American Power, 1991–2004," *Asian Survey* 45, no. 5 (2005): 667–686; Rosalie Chen, "China Perceives America: Perspectives of International Relations Experts," *Journal of Contemporary China* 12, no. 35 (2003): 285–297.

36. Philip Saunders, "China's America Watchers: Changing Attitudes toward the U.S.," *The China Quarterly* 161 (2000): 41–65.

37. Ian Johnson, "Test for New Leaders as Chinese Paper Takes on Censors," *The New York Times,* 6 January 2013.

38. Carsten Holz, "Have China Scholars All Been Bought?" *Far Eastern Economic Review,* 4 July 2007, p. 36. A recent study shows that overseas China scholars also face this "self-censorship" dilemma. See Sheena Chestnut Greitens and Rory Truex, "Repressive Experiences among China Scholars: New Evidence from Survey Data," 1 August 2018, available at SSRN: https://ssrn.com/abstract=3243059 or https://doi.org/10.2139/ssrn.3243059.

39. Li Wei and Song Yiming, "The Miniature of China's International Relations Research—the 'CCPSIS as a case study,'" in *Chinese Journal of International Politics*, no. 2, issue 2, 2017: 122–150. 李巍、宋亦明，"中国国际关系研究的缩影—以"政治学与国际关系共同体"会议为研究对象"，国际政治科学，2017 年第 2 卷第 2 期(总第 6 期)，第 122—150 页.

40. "US Public, Experts, Differ on China Policies," Carnegie Endowment for International Peace, 18 September 2012. https://carnegieendowment.org/publications/49411.

Following a similar methodology, the Center for Strategic and International Studies (CSIS) also conducted an opinion survey on "strategic elites" in 11 Asia Pacific economies in early 2014, which aimed to explore regional perceptual trend lines on power and order in Asia. However, the sample size of Chinese experts in this CSIS survey is only 35.

41. Despite our best efforts, we were unable to field our survey at the 11th CCPSIS annual meeting in 2018.
42. We include students in all of our analyses as most of them are in the MA and PhD programs of international relations and will soon become the next batch of Chinese IR scholars. Analytically, because nearly half of the respondents are students, dropping them would substantially reduce the statistical power and the significance of the temporal comparisons.

CHAPTER 2

On China's Power and the International Order: Is China a Challenger?

In international politics, power is a key concept for understanding the future contours of the world. As John Mearsheimer writes, "power is the currency of great-power politics, and states compete for it among themselves. What money is to economics, power is to international relations."[1] As China's power increases, speculations abound as to what China's rise will mean for the world's future. Will it bring tranquility or conflict? Although the Chinese government insists that its rise will be peaceful,[2] international relations (IR) scholars hold different views on the matter.

Some are optimistic, based on the contention that China's rise is within the existing international liberal order, and that China is becoming more socialized into the international system. John Ikenberry, for example, argues that China's rise will be constrained by the liberal international order, which will endure despite the decline of US hegemony.[3] Others are more pessimistic, worrying that an increasingly powerful China may stumble into conflict with the United States, falling into "Thucydides's Trap"[4]—an inevitable war between the existing hegemon and a rising power during the power transition in the international system.[5]

In this chapter, we explore China's power and its implications through a perceptual lens. As William Wohlforth rightly points out, perceptions of power matter, because power influences international relations through the perceptions of those who act on behalf of the state.[6] In the analogy of

© The Author(s) 2019
H. Feng et al., *How China Sees the World*,
https://doi.org/10.1007/978-981-15-0482-2_2

Thucydides's Trap, "the rise of Athens and the *fear* [emphasis added] that this instilled in Sparta" made the Peloponnesian War inevitable.[7] Here, the fear is the product of the hegemon's perception of a rival's power.

Rather than measuring the fear of the hegemon, we focus on the potential challenger. Our goal is to explore whether Chinese leaders perceive China as powerful enough to challenge the hegemon and the existing international order. As we mentioned in Chap. 1, however, directly measuring Chinese leaders' perceptions does not seem a likely endeavor. Therefore, we examine the views of Chinese IR scholars as an approximation for understanding Chinese leaders' perceptions.

In our opinion surveys conducted between 2014 and 2017, we asked the Chinese Community of Political Science and International Studies (CCPSIS) participants to evaluate China's power capabilities in relation to the international system and the current hegemon—the United States. First, we examined Chinese IR scholars' perceptions of the structure of the international system, an indirect measure of China's power because the evaluation requires placing China in the context of the changing power dynamics in the international system. Second, we examined Chinese IR scholars' direct perceptions of how China's power compares with that of the United States in various dimensions, including economic, military, cultural, political, and comprehensive power. Finally, we asked whether China poses a challenge to the current international order. We then complement the survey findings with textual analyses of Chinese IR scholars' publications in the top five Chinese IR journals in 2013–2018.

Through comparing our survey results and top scholarly publications, we provide a more complete assessment of what mainstream Chinese IR scholars think about China's power. These findings will also have policy implications. As scholars are the main medium between the public and the policy makers, an optimistic evaluation of China's power could reflect or inform the thinking of Chinese leaders and arouse nationalistic sentiments among the public, which in turn could encourage the Chinese government to take riskier actions against outside challenges, especially from the United States. Conversely, if our findings show that Chinese IR scholars have a more pessimistic view of China's power and its potential to challenge the existing international order, it would be counterproductive and even dangerous for other countries to view China as such.

The chapter has three sections. First, we present our survey results on Chinese IR scholars' perceptions about the structure of the international system, as well as China's power capabilities in various dimensions and in reference to the United States. Second, we discuss what the scholarly publications during the same time period reveal about Chinese IR scholars' perceptions and how they compare with the survey results. We conclude with a summary of this chapter's main findings.

China's Power Capabilities in the Four-Year Surveys

The International System: One Superpower Remains

After the end of the Cold War, Chinese IR scholars have been debating whether the world is moving toward multipolarity or has remained a unipolar system.[8] With China's power increasing, many see it taking on a larger role in the region and world.[9] Since China overtook Japan in 2010 as the world's second-largest economy, the moniker "G2," which indicates a bipolar world, has gained much more traction among both pundits and policy analysts.[10] Some even see China overtaking the United States soon in all power aspects.[11] Do Chinese IR scholars' views reflect this general perception?

To find out, in the survey we asked participants at the CCPSIS annual conferences how they would characterize the structure of the international system (guoji geju 国际格局). Figure 2.1 plots the responses to this question, both aggregated across the four years and by the individual sur-

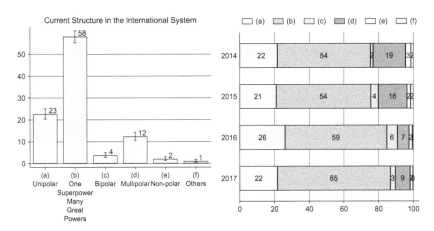

Fig. 2.1 Perceptions of the international system. Note: The left panel plots the distribution of the responses with 95% confidence intervals over the four-year period. The right panel plots the responses in each individual year of the survey. The numbers are in percentage points and may not add up to 100 due to rounding

vey year. Overall, we can see in the left panel of Fig. 2.1 that the majority of Chinese IR scholars (81%) view the United States as the only hegemon in the world. They disagree, however, on how long the unipolarity will last—58% describe the current international system as "one superpower with many great powers likely to catch up or overtake the superpower in the short run," and 23% believe that the superpower will not be replaced by other great powers. Another 12% consider the current world system multipolar. The rest of the responses are "bipolar" (4%), "non-polar" (2%), and "other" (1%).

The right panel of Fig. 2.1 plots the responses over time. Here we can see that while Chinese IR scholars acknowledge the absolute domination of the United States in the short term, they also view its power as slowly declining and the world moving toward multipolarity. In the first two years of our survey, the responses were remarkably similar. But things started to change in 2016. While respondents were relatively optimistic about the world shifting toward multipolarity (19% in 2014 and 16% in 2015), the proportions dropped to 7% in 2016 and 9% in 2017, and the differences are all statistically significant ($p < 0.001$ for all four pairwise comparisons).[12] The year 2017 is particularly interesting, as we see a significant jump from the previous three years in the number of respondents perceiving the international system as one superpower and many great powers, from 54% in 2014 and 2015 to 65% in 2017 ($p < 0.01$).

The question on the structure of the international system can give us some ideas about how China may be perceived in the system, particularly versus the hegemon, but we can also gauge this more directly. Figure 2.2 plots the responses to the question asking respondents to evaluate the power status of China in the international system. Overall, the survey participants showed a strong sense of confidence about China's rising power and influence in the region as well as in the world. Nearly half (46%) considered China a "rising superpower." The same proportion said that China is either an "Asian regional hegemon" (9%) or a rising one (37%).

A similar pattern emerges when we look at the responses over time. In 2016, there was a big drop from the previous two years in the proportion of participants perceiving China as a rising superpower, down from 44% in 2014 and 47% in 2015 to 37% in 2016, with the difference between 2015 and 2016 being statistically significant ($p < 0.01$). Meanwhile, a significantly higher proportion of scholars viewed China as an Asian regional hegemon (13%, $p < 0.05$) or a rising one in 2016 (45%, $p < 0.05$). This adjustment in self-perception regarding China's domain of influence—

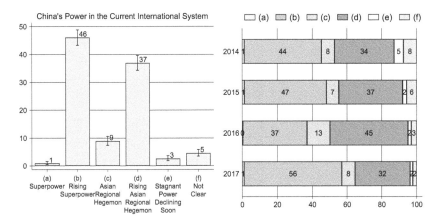

Fig. 2.2 Perceptions of China's power and status. Note: The left panel plots the distribution of the responses with 95% confidence intervals over the four-year period. The right panel plots the responses in each individual year of the survey. The numbers are in percentage points and may not add up to 100 due to rounding

from the whole world to the Asian region—suggests that Chinese IR scholars somehow downgraded China's potential influence on the global stage, becoming more skeptical of China's ability to compete with the United States. Considering the highly uncertain strategic environment in the world in 2016, such as the South China Sea flare-ups and the Hague ruling, it is not difficult to understand the emergence of a more self-constrained perception due to certain difficulties and even setbacks in China's foreign relations.

The perceptions of Chinese IR scholars swung in the opposite direction in 2017. As can be seen in the right panel of Fig. 2.2, there was a significant increase in the proportions of respondents who perceived China as a rising superpower (from 37% in 2016 to 56% in 2017, $p < 0.001$). This shift might have been the result of a rise in domestic nationalism and a heightened level of confidence about China facing the then-new US President, Donald Trump, whose "America First" policy was to shun American international leadership in the world.

In addition to asking respondents about their views on China's status in the international system, we also posed the same question regarding the United States. The results are displayed in Fig. 2.3. Consistent with the findings presented in the previous two figures, the aggregate responses

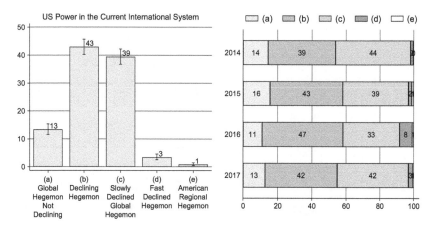

Fig. 2.3 Perceptions of US power and status. Note: The left panel plots the distribution of the responses with 95% confidence intervals over the four-year period. The right panel plots the responses in each individual year of the survey. The numbers are in percentage points and may not add up to 100 due to rounding

from the four-year surveys show China's IR scholars expressing near unanimity that the United States is the global hegemon. However, they disagree on whether and how much the United States is in decline because power is a relative term in world politics.[13] Over half of the respondents view the United States as the undisputed global hegemon with either no sign of declining (13%) or possible decline in the future (43%). On the other end of the spectrum are respondents who believe the United States is already declining, at either a slow (39%) or a fast (3%) pace.

Similar to responses to the question on China, answers indicated that perceptions of US status shifted over time. In 2016, there was a decrease in the proportion of participants who perceived the United States as a slowly declining hegemon (from 44% in 2014 to 33% in 2016, $p < 0.001$), with more considering the United States still a hegemon but in decline (from 39% in 2014 to 47% in 2016, $p = 0.05$). In the following year, the changes in the perceptions reversed, with more respondents believing the United States to be in a slow decline (from 33% to 42%, $p < 0.05$) and fewer indicating a fast decline (from 8% to 3%, $p = 0.001$).

Taken together, the responses to these three questions reveal an interesting finding regarding China's power and status in the eyes of Chinese IR scholars. On the one hand, they were generally confident about China's rise in the international system, despite some diplomatic setbacks in 2016. On the other hand, they were also fully aware that the world was and will remain unipolar, although there was a certain degree of optimism that the United States is already or will be in decline. These seemingly contradictory findings regarding China's rise and America's decline suggest that Chinese IR scholars held a realistic view of China's power capabilities versus the United States in that they did not believe China will replace the United States as the hegemon in the international system anytime soon. In other words, the consensus seems to be that a power transition between China and the United States will eventually happen, but not in the short term.

China's Hard and Soft Power

One potential explanation for the incongruity between Chinese IR scholars' perceptions of Chinese and American power in the international system is that the concept of power in international relations is multidimensional. Respondents could have been thinking about different dimensions of power when evaluating the positions of the two countries. To see whether this was indeed the case, in the survey we included a number of questions to measure respondents' views on different dimensions of China's power.

We categorize power into five areas: economic power, military power, political power, cultural power, and comprehensive power. Economic and military power are commonly treated as the major components of hard power, while political and cultural power belong to a state's soft power. Comprehensive power is a unique measurement of power, adopted by the Chinese government, which refers to a combination of the different dimensions of national power.[14] In the survey, we framed the relevant questions prospectively and comparatively, asking whether or not respondents believed that China's power in each of these dimensions will overtake America's in ten years. The answer choices were: "very likely," "likely," "not likely," "very unlikely," and "not clear."

We start by looking at economic power, which is the most significant and visible indicator of China's rise and perhaps the most likely dimension in which China could overtake the United States—in fact, some analysts proclaim the transition has already occurred.[15] Not surprisingly, our respondents seemed to agree, which can be seen in Fig. 2.4. Over half of the surveyed IR scholars believed it to be very likely (16%) or likely (40%) that China will pass the United States in terms of economic power.

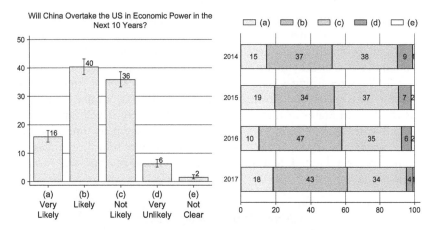

Fig. 2.4   China's economic power versus America's in ten years. Note: The left panel plots the distribution of the responses with 95% confidence intervals over the four-year period. The right panel plots the responses in each individual year of the survey. The numbers are in percentage points and may not add up to 100 due to rounding

The level of optimism about whether China's economic power will overtake America's grew over time, from 52% in 2014 to 61% in 2017 (combining the "very likely" and "likely" responses), and the difference is statistically significant ($p < 0.05$). This may not be surprising, given that during the same period, the Chinese government initiated the "Made in China 2025" project, launched the Belt and Road Initiative, and expanded its aid and investment in the developing world. All of these new endeavors might have boosted domestic confidence about China's power in the economic arena. However, it is worth pointing out that in our four-year surveys, a shrinking but still sizable proportion of respondents (38% in 2017) found it unlikely or very unlikely that China's economic power could surpass that of the United States.

Chinese IR scholars were decidedly less optimistic regarding the other aspect of hard power: an overwhelming majority (79%) of our respondents was convinced that China would be unlikely or very unlikely to overtake the United States in the military domain anytime soon (Fig. 2.5). This changed slowly over time, though, with more participants (21% in 2016 and 24% in 2017) saying that Chinese military power was very likely or likely to surpass America's, significant increases from the previous two years (14% in 2014 and 15% in 2015, $p < 0.05$). These results indicate a

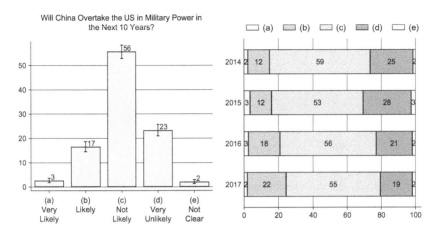

Fig. 2.5 China's military power versus America's in ten years. Note: The left panel plots the distribution of the responses with 95% confidence intervals over the four-year period. The right panel plots the responses in each individual year of the survey. The numbers are in percentage points and may not add up to 100 due to rounding

cautiously increasing confidence in Chinese military power, which might be explained by China's significant military build-ups in 2016 and 2017, including the deployment of its first aircraft carrier during this time.[16]

The Chinese government has emphasized boosting its soft power since the Hu Jintao era.[17] Over the last decade, Beijing has spent billions of dollars to promote Chinese soft power through its Confucius Institutes and other outreach programs throughout the world. Is this "charm offensive" working? Our next two survey questions look at two aspects of China's soft power. First, on the attractiveness of the Chinese political system versus that of the United States (Fig. 2.6), 73% of the respondents believed that China is unlikely or very unlikely to surpass the United States in terms of its political power, suggesting an implicit lack of confidence in the Chinese political system. Nevertheless, it should be noted that around one-quarter of respondents did believe the Chinese political system to be superior and opined that it could overtake America's in the next ten years. Moving on to the question of whether Chinese cultural power could overtake its US counterpart in the next ten years, we see an equally pessimistic view that persisted throughout the survey years: 70% of respondents believed it to be unlikely or very unlikely for China to surpass the United States in terms of cultural power, while only 24% thought otherwise (Fig. 2.7).

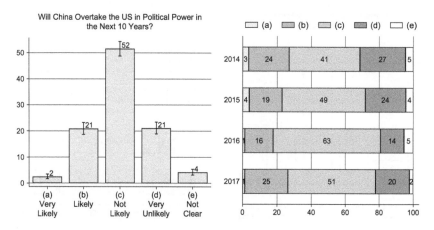

Fig. 2.6 China's political power versus America's in ten years. Note: The left panel plots the distribution of the responses with 95% confidence intervals over the four-year period. The right panel plots the responses in each individual year of the survey. The numbers are in percentage points and may not add up to 100 due to rounding

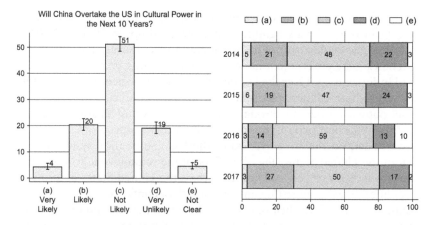

Fig. 2.7 China's cultural power versus America's in ten years. Note: The left panel plots the distribution of the responses with 95% confidence intervals over the four-year period. The right panel plots the responses in each individual year of the survey. The numbers are in percentage points and may not add up to 100 due to rounding

Consistent with the pattern regarding hard power, perceptions of Chinese soft power on both dimensions shifted over time. In 2014 and 2015, 27% and 23% of the respondents perceived the Chinese political system as likely or very likely to overtake the US system (Fig. 2.6). This dropped significantly to 17% in 2016 ($p < 0.05$) but bounced back to 26% in 2017 ($p < 0.05$). Similarly, in 2016 (Fig. 2.7), only 17% believed that China could overtake the United States in cultural power (combining the "very likely" and "likely" responses), versus 26% in 2014 and 25% in 2015 ($p < 0.05$). In 2017, this proportion almost doubled, reaching 30% ($p < 0.01$).

These shifting attitudes could be a result of the external environment. As we mentioned earlier, China's foreign policy encountered a number of setbacks in 2016, which could have dampened confidence in China's soft power. However, Trump's rise might have reversed this course because Trump's electoral victory is widely seen as a sign of America's democracy regressing. This possibility is further boosted by President Xi Jinping's active promotion of Chinese culture, embodied in the "China Dream." Still, it is clear that the majority of Chinese IR scholars are well aware of the limitations of China's soft power compared to America's.

Our last question was about comprehensive power. As mentioned above, this is a unique term that the Chinese government has used to evaluate its own power in the world. As Qi Haixia suggests, different researchers and research institutions have different standards and methods of calculating Chinese "comprehensive power."[18] In our surveys, we intended to measure the general attitude of Chinese IR scholars toward China's comprehensive power without relating this to any debates over methodological issues.

The results, displayed in Fig. 2.8, show that a large majority (81%) of the conference participants found it unlikely that China's comprehensive power could overtake America's. Once again, changes occurred in the last two survey years. When we combine the "very (un)likely" and "(un)likely" categories, the distributions of the responses were similar in the first three survey years. However, in 2016, fewer chose "very unlikely" (18%) and more selected "unlikely" (65%) than in previous years ($p < 0.05$). This slightly more optimistic outlook continued into the following year, which saw a significant surge in the proportion of positive responses ($p < 0.01$).

To summarize, our survey data suggest that Chinese IR scholars hold an unbalanced yet realistic view on China's power compared to America's. They are relatively optimistic about China's economic power

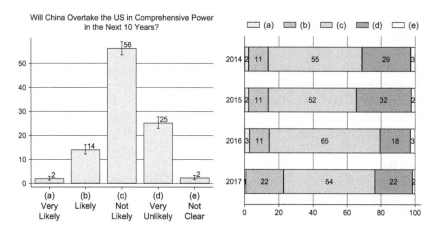

Fig. 2.8 China's comprehensive power versus America's in ten years. Note: The left panel plots the distribution of the responses with 95% confidence intervals over the four-year period. The right panel plots the responses in each individual year of the survey. The numbers are in percentage points and may not add up to 100 due to rounding

and cautiously optimistic about its comprehensive power, but not so much when it comes to military power and soft power. These findings are consistent with our previous conclusion that Chinese IR scholars did not buy into the idea of a power transition between China and the United States. Although they believed in China's rise, most of them still viewed the United States to be the sole superpower in the international system and felt it will likely take a long time for China to catch up.

Is China a Challenger to the World Order?

It is true that power matters in international politics. However, how China will use its power is even more important than how much power it possesses. Some Western scholars, such as Mearsheimer and Friedberg, strongly believe that China will use its increasing power to challenge US hegemony as well as the US-led liberal international order.[19] In the survey, we gauged this possibility by directly asking our respondents whether they believed China to be a challenger to the existing international order.

Figure 2.9 displays the results for the three years when the question was asked (2015–2017). Overall, two-thirds of the respondents disagreed that

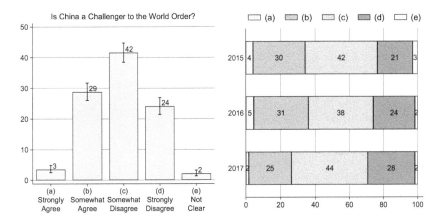

Fig. 2.9 Perceptions of China as a challenger to the world order. Note: The left panel plots the distribution of the responses with 95% confidence intervals over the four-year period. The right panel plots the responses in each individual year of the survey. The numbers are in percentage points and may not add up to 100 due to rounding

China is challenging the existing international order, while one-third agreed. The year 2017 once again stands out, as significantly more respondents disagreed with the statement that China is a challenger to the international order (72%, combining the "somewhat disagree" and "strongly disagree" categories) than in the previous two years (62% in 2016 and 63% in 2015, $p < 0.05$). This doesn't seem to square too well with results from above, which show our respondents in the same year becoming more confident about China's rising power and the relative decline of the United States. One interpretation is that for Chinese IR scholars, it is not a zero-sum game between China and the United States, and China's rise is not at the expense of US decline. This line of reasoning also echoes the official discourse of the Chinese government, which has repeatedly claimed that China is a beneficiary of the post-war international order and thus has no reason to overthrow the international system, even with its growing power capabilities.

It is worth noting that those respondents most confident of China's power do see China as a challenger. Figure 2.10 plots the coefficient estimates from a series of logistic regression models predicting the likelihood that a respondent would strongly agree with the statement that China is

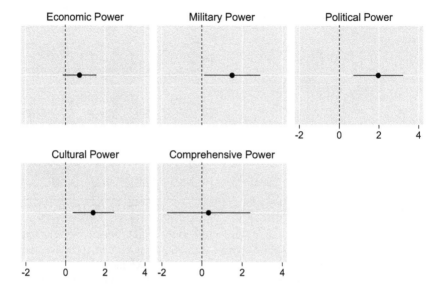

Fig. 2.10 Perceptions of China's power and the likelihood of China challenging the existing world order. Notes: The dots are point estimators from logistic regression models predicting the likelihood that a respondent would strongly agree that China is a challenger to the existing international order, using their perceptions of power and other sociodemographic variables (not shown). The horizontal bars are 95% confidence intervals

challenging the existing international order. The key independent variable is whether or not the respondent believes that China is very likely to overtake the United States in the next ten years in the five dimensions of power. Also included in the model but not reported in Fig. 2.10 are the sociodemographic variables of the respondents. The point estimators in all five models are positive, and three of them (military, political, and cultural power) are statistically significant. Fortunately, only an increasingly smaller minority of our respondents fall into this category.

CHINESE SCHOLARLY PUBLICATIONS ON CHINA'S POWER

In this section, we complement the findings from our four-year surveys by examining the views represented in the writings of Chinese IR scholars in the five leading Chinese IR journals, as described in Chap. 1.

On the Future International System

Regarding the structure of the international system, most of the publications on the topic suggest that the world is moving toward multipolarity, but the process could be protracted, troublesome, unbalanced, and bumpy.[20] Starting in 2013, most Chinese IR scholars have agreed in their written work that the international system has become "one superpower and many major powers" (一超多强)—with the United States as the superpower and China as one of the major powers. But scholars also argue that within this system, there could be different and fast-changing dynamics, most of which have to do with China's rise. For example, Feng Yujun points out that although the United States remains the dominant power in the world, its power has declined since the 2008 global financial crisis, facing particularly serious challenges in US-led political and economic institutions. This could be a sign that the US-led international system is loosening.[21]

Although recognizing that US power is in decline, scholars have also come to realize that in the coming decades, the United States will remain the most powerful country in the world.[22] Some scholars have written that the United States is no longer the "superpower" but rather the most powerful of the major poles. In the future world order, it will be difficult for one power to dominate the international system. For some scholars, a multipolar world does not mean an even, balanced power distribution among the major powers but rather an uneven, imbalanced one in which some nations are more powerful than others.[23]

Some Chinese scholars envision a G2 structure. For example, Zhou Fangyin argues that the power gap between China and the United States will gradually narrow, although the United States will remain the most powerful state in the international system. Concurrently, the power gap between China and powerful nations other than the United States will likely widen. In other words, the future international system will be a bipolar one in which the United States and China will dominate the two poles while other powers will lag behind.[24]

One interesting trend from scholarly publications is that Chinese IR scholars are inclined to link China's rise with the rise of developing countries, especially emerging powers. For example, Wang Fan suggests that the rise of emerging economies, including the BRICS (Brazil, Russia, India, China and South Africa) countries, has become a new feature of the international system.[25] Yang Jiemian summarizes the two characteristics of the international system as the rise of the East and the decline of the West (东升西降) as well as the ascent of the South and the fall of the North (南上北下).[26]

In sum, the views presented in the top five Chinese journals in our sample across five years are generally consistent with our survey findings on China's power in the international system. On the one hand, Chinese scholars are optimistic about the future direction of China's rise—that is, China will be able to play a major role in line with its power status. On the other hand, there is a shared understanding of the harsh reality that US dominance will remain but in a different form. In other words, Chinese IR scholars have a seemingly contradictory view of China's power and the future international system, and they do not see China's rise and America's decline as a zero-sum game.[27]

On the Different Components of China's Power

Reviewing the publications of Chinese IR scholars suggests that they have a clear perception regarding the different components of China's power versus that of the United States. Most scholars believe that China's rise in economic power is a fact but does not mean that China has become the second most powerful state in the world. As Chu Shulong notes, "Even though China is the second largest economy, when it comes to comprehensive power, China still lags far behind the developed countries. China also lacks soft power. As a result, in the international system, China's constructive role is limited."[28]

Fu Mengzi also acknowledges that even if China can become the number one economy in the near future, it will take a very long time for China to transfer from an economic power to a real comprehensive power in the world, which is measured by capabilities in the economy, technology, the military, and so forth.[29] Some scholars further contend that China is only a regional power in the Asia Pacific but not a global power per se.[30] Others also highlight the difference between China's GDP and GDP per capita in their calculation of power. For example, Zhang Qingmin argues that although China's GDP has become the second largest in the world, its GDP per capita only ranks 80th in the world. Therefore, China is at most the largest developing country; this defines its global role and identity, which will not change in the near future.[31]

On soft power, Chinese IR scholars recognize that China's soft power is still lagging behind America's, and they have proposed ways in which

China could further promote its soft power through contributing to global governance. For example, Bo Yan argues that China can promote its soft power by initiating a "China plan" with better designed cooperative and negotiation skills in the arena of global climate change.[32] In a similar vein, Li Yang and Huang Yanxi suggest that China should consider providing more international public goods to boost its soft power.[33] Zhang Yuyan argues that there are three sources of China's power and national rejuvenation: internationalizing China's currency (the renminbi yuan); participating in rule-making in global governance; and garnering respect for Eastern values and Chinese culture.[34]

One interesting finding from the Chinese scholarly journals is that there is very limited discussion on China's political power and cultural power in comparison with America's. Most scholarly publications focus on China's economic power, military power, soft power, and comprehensive power in general. There would seem to be two possible explanations for the lack of attention to China's political and cultural power. On the one hand, Chinese scholars might be including political and cultural power in their discussions of soft power. In other words, in the eyes of Chinese IR scholars, there is no need to separate political and cultural power from soft power. On the other hand, they might be trying to avoid discussing the Chinese political system in written publications because it is still a sensitive topic in Chinese academia.

Overall, the scholarly publications during this period show that Chinese IR scholars generally recognize the fact that China's comprehensive power is increasing but remains far behind that of the United States, which has not shown any real decline.[35] The reasons proposed for this gap in power include the dominant role of the US dollar in the financial sector,[36] America's modern nuclear weapons and anti-missile system, a global precision guidance system, and its dominant role in cyber space, intelligence, alliances, and geostrategic power.[37]

On the International Order

The international order is a hot topic in the writings of Chinese IR scholars. A close examination of their scholarly publications reveals two divergent arguments on the relationship between China and the international order. Some scholars argue that China has played an important role in building the current international order; downplaying the importance of the United States in establishing the post-war international order, they instead credit this to the United Nations and view China as part of that process.[38]

Other scholars argue that the current international order needs to be reformed and reshaped, and that China should play an important role in this process. For example, Gao Zugui argues that while China strongly supports the current international order based on the UN Charter, it should also actively refashion the international order to make it fairer and more democratic for all states in the world.[39] Similarly, Fu Mengzi points out that with increased power, China can no longer remain a rule-taker in the existing international order. Instead, it should pay more attention to participating in international institutions and play a more active role in their reform.[40]

Some scholars also highlight China's changing attitudes toward international institutions. As Zhang Chunman points out, China's early stance was generally aloof and sometimes even antagonistic, but its attitude has shifted over time after it began to participate more actively in the 1990s, culminating in its entry to the World Trade Organization (WTO).[41] In a similar vein, Lin Hongyu suggests that since 2001, China has entered a "full participation" stage, in which it has a better understanding of the essence of global governance and has learnt about how to utilize the rules and institutions of the current international order to fulfill its own national interests.[42]

It is interesting to note that Chinese IR scholars seem reluctant to use the word "challenger" when describing the relationship between China and the current international order. This contrasts with the findings in our survey, suggesting that respondents may be more willing to speak their minds under anonymity. Further, in publications, they also avoid linking the current international order with US leadership. Instead, they are more likely to describe China as a "participant" and a "reformer" in the current international order. One such example is Feng Yujun, who states that China's 30-year development has greatly benefited from its engagement in the current international order. As a result, China is a participating and constructive member, not a challenger or subverter of the current international order.[43]

Although most scholars acknowledge that China needs to play a more important role in reshaping or reforming the current international order, they disagree on what China should do. Some believe China is still a relatively new player on the international stage and thus needs to learn how to play by the rules while increasing its voice by acquiring more "discourse power" or "narrative power."[44] Others, however, adopt a more aggressive stance and argue that the current international order includes some "unfair" rules and norms, so China will need to work with other developing countries to reform these unjust aspects.[45] Some even suggest that China should be prepared to "build a new kitchen"—that is, to create new institutions for a new international order if it fails in its efforts to reform the current one.[46]

There are also scholars who call for a middle ground, contending that China should not challenge the political and security domains of the international order, which are dominated by the United States. Instead, it should focus on strengthening its leadership in the economic and financial aspects of the international order.[47] This "targeted reforming" approach is based on leveraging China's comparative advantage in the economic arena while avoiding a direct confrontation with the United States.

CONCLUSION

In this chapter, we have presented findings from our four-year survey on Chinese IR scholars' perceptions about China's power capabilities. In addition, we have examined publications in the top five Chinese IR journals on the same question. On China's power, we find that most Chinese IR scholars hold a seemingly contradictory but realistic view of its capabilities in the international system. Although they are optimistic about China's rise, especially as an Asian regional power, they do not perceive a rapid decline of the United States in the foreseeable future, nor do they envision China overtaking the United States in terms of its economic, military, political, cultural, and comprehensive power. In other words, they do not see a zero-sum game between the rise of China and the decline of the United States, contrary to what power transition realists have argued for a long time. These views are reflected in their scholarly publications, where the general consensus is that the future international system will comprise "one superpower and many great powers," with China as only one of the great powers.

Regarding China's relationship within the current international order, both our survey results and our textual analyses of scholarly publications show that Chinese scholars do not perceive a confrontation between China and the outside world. Instead, they believe that China's development largely depends on its engagement with the international order, although they are reluctant to link US leadership with the post-war international order. Chinese scholars advocate a reforming role for China, whereby it would reshape the international order from inside instead of challenging or overthrowing the international order from outside.

Regardless of how China intends to change or reform the international order, one unavoidable challenge is how to cope with the United States, the dominant power or hegemon in the current international system. Our next chapter will take a closer look at China's bilateral relations with the United States through the eyes of China's IR scholars.

Notes

1. John J. Mearsheimer, *The Tragedy of Great Power Politics* (New York: W.W. Norton & Company, 2001).
2. Zheng Bijian, "China's 'Peaceful Rise' to Great-Power Status," *Foreign Affairs* 84, no. 5 (2005): 18–24.
3. G. John Ikenberry, "The Rise of China and the Future of the West—Can the Liberal System Survive," *Foreign Affairs* 87, no. 1 (2008): 2–22.
4. Graham Allison, *Destined for War: Can America and China Escape Thucydides's Trap?* (Boston: Houghton Mifflin Harcourt, 2017).
5. Abramo F.K. Organski, *World Politics* (New York: Knopf, 1958); Abramo F.K. Organski and Jacek Kugler, *The War Ledger* (Chicago: University of Chicago Press, 2015).
6. William C. Wohlforth, "The Perception of Power: Russia in the pre-1914 Balance," *World Politics* 39, no. 3 (1987): 353–381.
7. Allison, *Destined for War*, 27, quoting an English translation of Thucydides.
8. Mao Weizhun, "Debating China's International Responsibility," *Chinese Journal of International Politics* 9, no. 3 (2018): 349–374; Chen Zheng, "China Debates the Non-Interference Principle," *Chinese Journal of International Politics* 10, no. 2 (2018): 173–210.
9. David L. Shambaugh, *China Goes Global: The Partial Power*, vol. 111 (Oxford: Oxford University Press, 2013).
10. Prominent advocates include former National Security Advisor Zbigniew Brzezinski, historian Niall Ferguson, former World Bank President Robert Zoellick, and former chief economist Justin Yifu Lin.
11. Major points from the symposium: Li Meihua and Zhang Zhenting, "Constructing Northeast Asia Peace and Security Institutions—2015 Summit on Korean Peninsular Research" *Contemporary International Relations*, no. 5 (2015): 61–62. 李梅花、张振亭:《东北亚和平安全机制的构建—朝鲜半岛研究 2015 高峰论坛纪要》,《现代国际关系》 2015 年第 5 期, 第 61–62 页.; Zhou Fangyin, "Trends in Neighbourhood and China's Neighbourhood Strategic Choices," *Foreign Affairs Review*, no. 1 (2014): 29.

周方银: 《周边环境走向与中国的周边战略选择》, 《外交评论》 2014 年第 1 期, 第 29 页.

12. Unless noted otherwise, the p-values are based on two-tailed tests comparing the percentages of responses across the four years.

13. David A. Baldwin, *Power and International Relations: A Conceptual Approach* (Princeton: Princeton University Press, 2016).

14. Qi Haixia, "Disputing Chinese Views on Power," *The Chinese Journal of International Politics* 10, no. 2 (2017): 211–239.

15. Hu Angang, "On Super China," in Tsinghua University School of Public Policy's Report on China 2015 available at: http://www.sppm.tsinghua.edu.cn/xycbw/gqbg/26efe48960740c880160a0c07528001a.html. See also "Hu Angang Responding to 'China is passing the US in all aspects: with data on intellectual property rights data as evidence'" 1 April 2018. 胡鞍钢回应"中国全面超越美国"论: 有知识产权数据库做论证 http://www.guancha.cn/economy/2018_04_01_452304.shtml.

16. "China Launches its First Home-Built Aircraft Carrier," *The Guardian*, 26 April 2017, available at: https://www.theguardian.com/world/2017/apr/26/china-launches-second-aircraft-carrier-that-is-first-built-at-home.

17. Mingjiang Li, "China Debates Soft Power," *The Chinese Journal of International Politics* 2, no. 2 (2008): 287–308; Ding Sheng, "To Build a 'Harmonious World': China's Soft Power Wielding in the Global South," *Journal of Chinese Political Science* 13, no. 2 (2008): 193–213.

18. Qi Haixia, 2017, ibid.

19. Mearsheimer, John J. "China's unpeaceful rise." *CURRENT HISTORY-NEW YORK THEN PHILADELPHIA-* 105, no. 690 (2006): 160. Mearsheimer, John J. "The gathering storm: China's challenge to US power in Asia." *The Chinese Journal of International Politics* 3, no. 4 (2010): 381–396. Friedberg, Aaron L. "The future of US–China relations: Is conflict inevitable?" *International security* 30, no. 2 (2005): 7–45. Friedberg, Aaron L. "The debate over US China strategy." *Survival* 57, no. 3 (2015): 89–11.

20. Wu Zhicheng, "The International System Remains in the Process of Multipolarisation," *Contemporary International Relations*, no. 7 (2014): 11–13. 吴志成: 《国际体系仍然处于多极化进程中》, 《现代国际关系》 2014 年第7期, 第 11–13 页. Wu further pointed out that there is no substantial change in the comparative power status of major players in the system.

21. Feng Yujun, "Great Powers Strategic Competition in Great Transformation," *Contemporary International Relations*, no. 4 (2013): 10–12. 冯玉军: 《"大变局"下的大国战略竞争》, 《现代国际关系》 2013 年第 4 期, 第 10–12 页.

22. Zhang Yuyan, "Establishing Grand Strategy on National Interests," *Contemporary International Relations*, no. 10 (2013): 39–40. 张宇燕: 《以国家利益设定中国对外战略》,《现代国际关系》2013 年第 10 期, 第 39–40 页.

23. Xu Jian, "Historical Conditions and Major Difficulties in Constructing A New Type of Major Power Relations between the US and China," *China International Studies*, no. 2 (2013): 8–19. 徐坚: 《构建中美新型大国关系的历史条件与主要问题》,《国际问题研究》2013 年第 2 期, 第 8–19 页.; Lin Limin, "New Theory and New Thinking for Understanding the New International Transformation," *Contemporary International Relations*, no. 4 (2013): 29–30. 林利民: 《认识新一轮国际格局变化呼唤新理论、新思维》,《现代国际关系》2013 年第 4 期, 第 29–30 页.

24. Zhou Fangyin, "Trends in Neighbourhood and China's Neighbourhood Strategic Choices." 周方银: 《周边环境走向与中国的周边战略选择》,《外交评论》2014 年第1期, 第 29.

25. Wang Fan, "How to Judge and Sustain Strategic Opportunity," *China International Studies*, no. 5 (2018): 38. 王帆: 《战略机遇期的判断与维护》,《国际问题研究》2018 年第5期, 第 38 页.

26. Yang Jiemian, "China's New Strategic Thinking and Planning in Diplomacy in the New Era," *Foreign Affairs Review*, no. 1 (2018): 8. 杨洁勉: 《新时代中国外交的战略思维和谋划》,《外交评论》2018 年第 1 期, 第 8 页.

27. Ling Shengli, "Sub-Optimal Choice: US-China Competition for Leadership in the Asia Pacific," *Contemporary Asia Pacific*, no. 1 (2017): 109–138. 凌胜利: 《拒优战略: 中美亚太主导权竞争,《当代亚太》2017 年第 1 期, 第 109–138 页.; Tang Jian, "Power Transition and War: International System, National Model and China's Rise," *Contemporary Asia Pacific*, no. 3 (2014): 63–96; Wang Zaibang, "US-China Relationship in Transition: Some Observations and Thoughts," *Contemporary International Relations*, no. 11 (2015): 14–21. 王在邦: 《中美关系划时代转型的观察与思考》,《现代国际关系》2015 年第 11 期, 第 14–21 页. Zhu Feng, "Will Island building Change the South China Sea Reality?" *China International Studies*, no. 3 (2015): 7–20. 朱锋: 《岛礁建设会改变南海局势现状吗?》,《国际问题研究》2015 年第 3 期, 第 7–20 页.

28. Chu Shulong, "Analysis and Policy Research on China's Neighborhood Security Environment," *Contemporary International Relations*, no. 10 (2013): 7–9. 楚树龙: 《当前中国周边安全环境分析与对策研究》,《现代国际关系》2013 年第 10 期, 第 7–9 页.

29. Fu Mengzi, "China's Historical Position and Diplomatic Strategy in the New Era," *Contemporary International Relations*, no. 8 (2017): 4–6. 傅梦孜: 《新时期中国的历史方位与外交方略》,《现代国际关系》2017 年第 8 期, 第 4–6 页. See also Chu Shulong and Zhang Xiaoying, "How to Read and Analyze the Major Problems in US-China Relations," *Contemporary International Relations*, no. 7 (2016): 7–13. 楚树龙、章晓

英: 《对关于美国的几个重大问题的认识与判断》, 《现代国际关系》 2016 年第 7 期, 第 7–13 页.

30. Liu Feng, "Strategic Competition between US and China and the Security Situation of East Asia," *Contemporary International Relations*, no. 8 (2017): 23–30. 刘丰: 《中美战略竞争与东亚安全态势》, 《现代国际关系》 2017 年第 8 期, 第 23–30 页. Han Zhaoying and Huang Zhaolong, "China's Rise, East Asia Structure, and East Asian Order: Now and Future," *Contemporary International Relations*, no. 9 (2017): 1–10. 韩召颖、黄钊龙: 《中国崛起、东亚格局和东亚秩序: 现状与未来》, 《现代国际关系》 2017 年第 9 期, 第 1–10 页.

31. Zhang Qingmin, "Understanding Major Power Diplomacy with Chinese Characteristics," *World Economics and Politics*, no. 9 (2018): 74. 张清敏: 《理解中国特色大国外交》, 《世界经济与政治》 2018 年第 9 期, 第 74 页.

32. Bo Yan, "Will and Capability to Cooperate: A New Framework for Understanding China's Involvement in Global Climate Change Governance," *World Economics and Politics*, no. 1 (2013): 149–155. 薄燕: 《合作意愿与合作能力-一种分析中国参与全球气候变化治理的新框架》, 《世界政治与经济》 2013 年第 1 期, 第 149–155 页.

33. Li Yang and Huang Yanxi, "US-China Competition over Trade Regimes—A Look from the Angle of International Public Goods," *World Politics and Economics*, no. 10 (2016): 114. 李杨、黄艳希: 《中美国际贸易制度之争-基于国际公共产品提供的视角》, 《世界经济与政治》 2016 年第 10 期, 第 114 页.

34. Zhang Yuyan, "Roots of China's Economic Growth and China's National Rejuvenation," *World Politics and Economics*, no. 1 (2013): 1. 张宇燕: 《经济增长源泉与中华民族复兴》, 《世界政治与经济》 2013 年第 1 期, 第 1 页.

35. Feng Yujun, "New Changes in the International Situation and China's Strategic Choices," *Contemporary International Relations*, no. 3 (2017): 9–15. 冯玉军: 《国际形势新变化与中国的战略选择》, 《现代国际关系》 2017 年第 3 期, 第 9–15 页.

36. Li Wei, "The Hegemonic Role of the Dollar and RMB's Future," *Contemporary International Relations*, no. 9 (2016): 1–11. 李巍: 《美元的霸权与人民币的未来》, 《现代国际关系》 2016 年第 9 期, 第 1–11 页.

37. Yuan Peng, "Global Transformation and New World Order," *Contemporary International Relations*, no. 10 (2016): 1–5. 袁鹏: 《全球大变局与世界新秩序》, 《现代国际关系》 2016 年第 10 期, 第 1–5 页.

38. Yu Minyou, "The UN's role in post-War international order evolvement and China's contribution," *China International Studies*, no. 6 (2015): 9–22. 余敏友: 《联合国对战后国际秩序的发展与中国的贡献》, 《国际问题研究》 2015 年第 6 期, 第 9–22 页.

Lu Jing, "Analysis on the international responses to China's rise," *China International Studies*, no. 2 (2015): 31–46. 卢静: 《中国和平崛起的国际舆论环境分析》, 《国际问题研究》 2015 年第 2 期, 第 31–46 页. Wu Zhicheng, "The International System is still in the process of multipolarization," *Contemporary International Relations*, no. 7 (2014): 11–13. 吴志成: 《国际体系仍然处于多极化进程中》, 《现代国际关系》 2014 年第 7 期, 第 11–13 页.

39. Gao Zugui, "Characteristics and Trends in Contemporary International Strategic Environment," *China International Studies*, no. 6 (2015): 23–25. 高祖贵: 《当前国际战略环境特点与走势》, 《国际问题研究》 2015 年第 6 期, 第 23–35 页.

40. Fu Mengzi, "Thoughts on China's Peripheral Strategy," *Contemporary International Relations*, no. 10 (2013): 20–21. 傅梦孜: 《中国周边战略问题思考点滴》, 《现代国际关系》 2013 年第 10 期, 第 20–21 页.

41. Zhang Chunman, "From Comprehensive Denial to Selective Participation: Changes and Explanations of China's Attitude towards International Order," *Journal of Contemporary Asia-Pacific Studies*, no. 4 (2014): 27–46. 张春满: 《从全面去合法性到选择性嵌入: 冷战后中国对国际秩序的态度变迁及其解释》, 《当代亚太》 2014 年第 3 期, 第 27–46 页.

42. Lin Hongyu, "Evolution of China's Participation in the International Order," *Contemporary International Relations*, no. 7 (2014): 28–30. 林宏宇: 《中国参与国际秩序的历史进程》, 《现代国际关系》 2014 年第 7 期, 第 28–30 页.

43. Feng Yujun, "New Changes in the International Situation and China's Strategic Choices." 冯玉军: 《国际形势新变化与中国的战略选择》, 《现代国际关系》 2017 年第 3 期, 第 9–15 页.

44. See the works by Shi Yinhong, Zhao Xiaochun, Wang Yizhou, Hu Shisheng, Lin Hongyu, and Liu Xiaoying, *Contemporary International Relations*, no. 7 (2014).

45. Wang Fan, "Major Power Diplomacy with Chinese Characteristics: Challenges and Strategic Choices," *Contemporary International Relations*, no. 8 (2017): 8–11. 王帆: 《中国特色大国外交: 挑战与战略选择》, 《现代国际关系》 2017 年第 8 期, 第 8–11 页.

46. Zhang Yuncheng, "A Brief Analysis of the World Economic System 'Rebalance'," *Contemporary International Relations*, no. 7 (2014): 23–25. 张运成: 《简析世界经济体系"再平衡"》, 《现代国际关系》 2014 年第 7 期, 第 23–25 页.

47. Ling Shengli, "Sub-Optimal Choice: China and the US Leadership Competition in the Asia Pacific." 凌胜利: 《拒优战略: 中美亚太主导权竞争》, 《当代亚太》 2017 年第 1 期, 第 109–138 页.

CHAPTER 3

On US–China Relations: Problems and Prospects

The US–China relationship is currently the world's most complicated bilateral relationship, yet the one with the most potential impact on the future of international politics in the twenty-first century. Chinese elites and policy makers have always identified the US–China relationship as the most important one in China's foreign relations.[1] How China develops its foreign policy toward the United States is largely shaped by how Chinese leaders perceive the United States as well as US policy toward China. In the studies of US–China relations, it has long been a tradition to examine the perceptions of "America watchers" in China and use their views to shed light on what China's leaders think about the United States.[2]

In this chapter, we follow this research tradition to examine Chinese international relations (IR) scholars' perceptions of the US–China relations through our "opinion survey–textual analysis" approach. In the surveys, we examined (1) how scholars assess current and future US–China relations; (2) how they perceive the major challenges and areas of common interest in this bilateral relationship; and (3) their opinions on America's role in China's territorial disputes with its neighbors. We then complement the survey findings by comparing and contrasting them with the scholarly articles published on these topics in the top Chinese IR journals.

Many scholars and analysts have pointed out that domestic political cycles in the United States often drive US–China relations. A common pattern since Reagan involves each new president criticizing the

© The Author(s) 2019
H. Feng et al., *How China Sees the World*,
https://doi.org/10.1007/978-981-15-0482-2_3

predecessor's policy toward China and taking tougher positions regarding issues of security (for Republicans) or trade and human rights (for Democrats), which strain the bilateral relations, only to become more pragmatic after overcoming the initial "learning curve" and finding common ground on which to work with China; this helps improve relations until a new president comes in.

The four-year time frame of our surveys coincides with the transition from the Obama to the Trump administration. The latter seems to have broken away from the previous pattern, engaging in an ongoing trade war that shows no sign of resolution in the foreseeable future. Even though our last survey was conducted before the trade war, tracing the responses over time allows us to see how the perceptions of Chinese IR scholars (and to some extent Chinese leaders) have evolved during this period and whether these groups are prepared for a possible paradigm shift in US–China relations.

There are three sections in this chapter. First, we present the results from our four-year surveys, which suggest that a majority of Chinese IR scholars hold a neutral view on bilateral relations. The surveys also show most scholars agree that the biggest challenges are security issues, particularly in the South China Sea and the Taiwan Strait, but they also see many areas of common interest where the two countries can work together. In the second section, we use the sample of Chinese scholarly publications to examine mainstream views on the relationship. This analysis strengthens and enriches our understanding of Chinese scholars' perceptions of US–China relations. It also reveals some nuanced debates among these scholars on the future of US–China relations. In the concluding section, we discuss the policy implications of our findings for the study of US–China relations.

FOUR-YEAR SURVEYS: CAUTIOUS VIEWS ON US–CHINA RELATIONS

It is perhaps not an exaggeration to say that for many Chinese IR scholars, the most important foreign policy question facing China today is its relationship with the United States. Each year at the Chinese Community of Political Science and International Studies (CCPSIS) annual conference, at least 10% of the panels and papers are devoted exclusively to analyses of US–China relations, and many more to the theoretical and policy implications of these relations for a broader range of issues. This is also reflected in our surveys. As we showed in Chap. 2, we designed the questions on China's power and its position in the international system in reference to the United States.

In this section, we take a closer look at how Chinese IR scholars evaluate this important relationship, using three sets of questions in the survey that gauge CCPSIS participants' perceptions of current and future US–China relations, the countries' common interests and challenges, and possible US intervention in China's territorial disputes with its neighbors.

US–China Relations Now and Into the Future

In the survey, we asked respondents how they would describe US–China relations now and in ten years. The potential answers were "very good," "good," "neither good nor bad," "antagonistic," and "not clear." We first look at their evaluations of the current relationship, which are plotted in Fig. 3.1. Overall, the vast majority (71%) of the surveyed scholars have a neutral view, describing the US–China relationship as neither good nor bad across the four years. The rest of the respondents are more optimistic

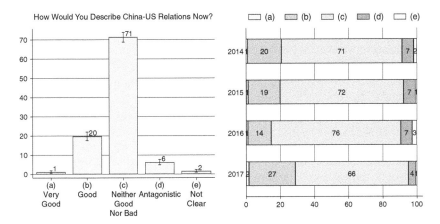

Fig. 3.1   Evaluation of current US–China relations. Note: The left panel plots the distribution of the responses with 95% confidence intervals over the four-year period. The right panel plots the responses in each individual year of the survey. The numbers are in percentage points and may not add up to 100 due to rounding

than pessimistic, with 21% saying that the relationship is very good or good and only 6% characterizing the relationship as antagonistic.

A number of findings are worth highlighting when we compare the results over time. First, the distributions of the responses in the first two years of the survey are almost identical. This suggests that the views on US–China relations among Chinese IR scholars were quite stable toward the last stretch of Obama's second term. Second, there was a statistically significant drop from 20% in 2014 to 15% in 2016 for those who perceived US–China relations to be very good or good, and a similar size of increase in the neutral responses ($p < 0.05$). This change is understandable because it was a US election year. Although foreign policy has never been a top issue in US presidential elections, the "China bashing" by presidential candidates from both parties seems to have cast a shadow on Chinese scholars' view of bilateral relations, though the number of respondents seeing the countries as outright adversaries remained small. Finally, after Trump emerged as the new president in 2017, the number of positive responses nearly doubled from 15% to 29% ($p < 0.001$). This surge in optimism most likely can be attributed to a honeymoon period between the two countries, especially after the Trump–Xi Mar-a-Lago summit in April 2017, three months before our survey was conducted.

Figure 3.2 plots the responses from the question on the long-term outlook of US–China relations in ten years. Compared to the previous question, a smaller majority of the respondents (60%) believed that the relationship would not get better or worse, while more respondents (26%) were hopeful that the future relationship would be good or very good. A similar pattern emerges when we compare the responses over time. In particular, the US election year sees a significant drop of 7% in the proportion of respondents perceiving future US–China relations as either very good or good from 2014 ($p < 0.05$). In the meantime, twice as many respondents expected the bilateral relations to deteriorate ($p < 0.01$) and three times as many were simply "unsure" of what the relationship would be like in ten years ($p < 0.001$).

In the following year, opinions regarding the future of the bilateral relationship improved to the same level as before the election; the distribution of the responses is statistically indistinguishable from the first two years of the survey under Obama. It appears that after the dust from the US election had settled and Chinese IR scholars had time to assess the new Trump presidency, their long-term outlook on US–China relations reverted to the pre-election equilibrium.

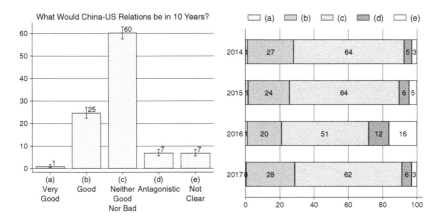

Fig. 3.2 Outlook of US–China relations in ten years. Note: The left panel plots the distribution of the responses with 95% confidence intervals over the four-year period. The right panel plots the responses in each individual year of the survey. The numbers are in percentage points and may not add up to 100 due to rounding

Major Challenges in US–China Relations

What do Chinese IR scholars see as major challenges in US–China relations? In the surveys, we listed nine commonly discussed issues: Taiwan, the South China Sea, democratic politics, US–China trade disputes, the Diaoyu/Senkaku Islands dispute, currency, Internet and cyber security, human rights, and energy and the environment. For each issue, we asked respondents whether they believed it to be a major challenge that could negatively affect bilateral relations. Respondents were also allowed to propose issues beyond the ones presented. Because only a handful of respondents did so, we focus our analyses on these nine issues.

Figure 3.3 illustrates these issues ranked in descending order from the most to the least challenging according to Chinese IR scholars over the four-year period. The first thing we notice is a bias toward "high politics"—three of the five most challenging issues are related to China's "core interests" of sovereignty and territorial integrity. In particular, about half of the respondents identified the Taiwan issue and the South China Sea dispute as the top two challenges. This is hardly surprising, as Taiwan has long been the most salient issue in US–China relations. Somewhat surprising is that more than twice as many respondents regarded the South

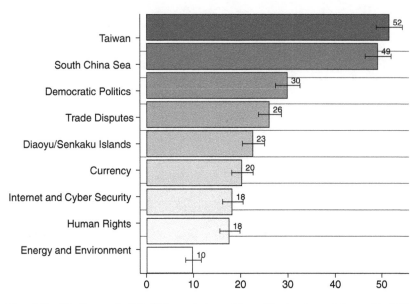

Fig. 3.3 Challenges in US–China relations. Note: The horizontal bars with 95% confidence intervals are percentages of respondents saying that the particular issue is a major challenge in US–China relations

China Sea as more challenging than the East China Sea, but this was likely due to there having been more recent tensions in the former than in the latter (more on this below).

The ideological differences between the political systems of the United States and China have been the root of friction between the two nations for a long time. The Chinese government often treats US efforts at promoting democracy in the world as a serious threat to China's regime security, which would explain why democratic politics was ranked the third most challenging issue, though it was selected by less than one-third of the participants (30%). This points to Chinese IR scholars' confidence in the resilience of China's political system.[3]

China's huge and growing trade surplus against the United States has long been a point of contention between the two countries, leading to dozens of disputes at the World Trade Organization (WTO) over the past two decades.[4] Nevertheless, only slightly more than one-quarter of the respondents (26%) believed that trade disputes between the two countries would undermine US–China relations. Related to trade disputes is the issue of China's alleged manipulation of its currency, which even fewer respondents (20%) regarded as a potential problem, possibly because China reformed its exchange regime in 2005 and dropped an explicit peg to the US dollar, leading to a slow but steady appreciation in value of the renminbi. The other "low-politics" issue—energy and the environment—received the fewest votes, selected by just 10% of the respondents.

Human rights used to be a major problem between the United States and China, especially during the 1990s, when Congress tried to use the granting of most-favored-nation (MFN) status as a way of pressuring China on its human rights abuses.[5] However, since the 2000s, the human rights issue has lost its significance in US–China relations. This does not mean that the United States has forgone its criticisms against China on the human rights front; on the contrary, Congress continues regularly to condemn China's human rights violations. However, our survey results suggest most Chinese IR scholars have come to understand that the human rights issue would not derail bilateral relations—only 18% of the surveyed participants considered it a major challenge.

The issue of Internet and cyber security has gained more saliency since the early 2010s, with the US media ramping up its coverage on the Chinese cyber threat over the years.[6] The US government has also accused the Chinese People's Liberation Army of stealing sensitive (military and business) information, and there have been cases of Chinese Americans arrested for cyber security-related criminal activities. The two countries initiated a formal bilateral dialogue in mid-2013 on these issues, but it was abruptly terminated in 2014.[7] In our surveys, the majority of the respondents (82%) did not view the cyber security issue as a major problem for bilateral relations. This will most likely change with the recent controversy over Huawei and the intensified technological competition between the two countries.

Figure 3.4 breaks down the responses by year. Similar to what emerged from the general evaluations of bilateral relations, the responses are quite stable in 2014 and 2015, and the ranking of the issues does not change much (Table 3.1). There are three exceptions. First, there is a statistically significant increase in the number of respondents choosing the South China Sea dispute ($p < 0.01$), making it the most challenging issue in 2015. It appears Chinese IR scholars were worried that China's land reclamation projects in the South China Sea, which began in the summer of 2014, could spark more tensions between the two countries. Second,

Fig. 3.4 Challenges in US–China relations by year. Note: The horizontal bars with 95% confidence intervals are percentages of respondents saying that the particular issue is a major challenge in US–China relations

Table 3.1 Ranking the challenges in US–China relations by year

	2014	*2015*	*2016*	*2017*
Taiwan	1	2	1	1
South China Sea	2	1	2	2
Democratic politics	3	3	3	4
Trade disputes	4	4	7	3
Diaoyu/Senkaku Islands	5	6	4	6
Human rights	8	8	5	5
Internet and cyber security	6	7	6	7
Currency	7	5	8	8
Energy and environment	9	9	9	9

more respondents took notice of the currency issue, likely because the US Congress was discussing the new Trade Facilitation and Trade Enforcement Act, a bipartisan effort aimed at penalizing countries determined to be currency manipulators. Finally, concerns over the Diaoyu/Senkaku Islands have eased, thanks to formal talks held between President Xi Jinping and Japanese Prime Minister Shinzo Abe in November 2014, the first such talks since the two leaders took office.

The uncertainties surrounding the 2016 US presidential election, in combination with a number of events that year, resulted in heightened apprehension among Chinese IR scholars over six of the nine issues, especially those in the realm of "high politics." In particular, a majority of the participants (65%) believed that Taiwan had become a major problem for US–China relations. This significant change ($p < 0.001$) was apparently a consequence of Taiwan's power transition from the nationalist party (Kuomintang) to the independently oriented Democratic Progressive Party in the 2016 presidential election. It reveals the deep-rooted concerns of Chinese elites over the Taiwan issue and its implications for future US–China relations.

Many Chinese IR scholars have blamed China's diplomatic difficulties in the South China Sea on the United States' "rebalance to Asia," which encouraged other claimants of the South China Sea to challenge China's position.[8] The double-digit increase from the previous year ($p < 0.001$) can be attributed to the pending ruling in the arbitration case brought by the Philippines in 2014 and to increased pressure from the United States.[9] The survey was conducted a few days before The Hague ruled in favor of the Philippines, an outcome that was largely expected. In addition, in October 2015, the United States began sending US Navy patrol ships near the artificial islands China built in the disputed Spratly and Paracel archipelagos, as part of America's Freedom of Navigation Operations (FONOPs).

Surprisingly, even though on the campaign trail, both US presidential candidates, and Trump in particular, lambasted China for its trade surplus against the US and for being a currency manipulator,[10] respondents in 2016 actually rolled back their concerns over these issues. This reflects a traditional view among Chinese IR scholars that economic ties can stabilize US–China bilateral relations, especially at times of uncertainty.

This optimism quickly dissipated in 2017, when Trump took the trade issue seriously, delivered his campaign promises to "make America Great again," and threatened to raise tariffs on steel and aluminum. Though these tariffs would affect many countries, it was apparent (and proven later) that the ultimate target was China. Consequently, the proportion of survey participants who thought "trade dispute" would be a major challenge nearly doubled from 19% in 2016 to 34% in 2017 ($p < 0.001$), propelling its rank among the nine issues from seventh to third.

Another big change in the 2017 survey followed President Rodrigo Duterte's rise to power in the Philippines in the summer of 2016, after which he skillfully, and also surprisingly, rebuilt the damaged relationship between the Philippines and China after the arbitration ruling. The subsequent relaxation of tensions in the South China Sea disputes was also facilitated by the Trump administration's temporary suspension of the FONOPs in the spring of 2017, in the hope of forcing China to increase pressure on North Korea. Hence, there was a good reason for the reduced urgency in the perceptions of Chinese participants regarding the South China Sea, though it still remained in the top two of the most challenging issues that could affect US–China relations.

Common Interests

In addition to major challenges facing US–China relations, we also asked participants to identify issues of common interest between the two countries. As with the question on major challenges, we provided respondents with nine issues, six of which were identical or similar to those in the previous question: Taiwan, trade, human rights, climate change, energy, and internet and cyber security. The other three were anti-terrorism, Non-Proliferation Treaty (NPT), and financial stability. Again, respondents had the option of offering additional issues, but we do not include these in the analyses due to the small number of respondents who did so.

Figure 3.5 plots the overall distribution of the responses during the four-year period, which can be divided into three categories. First, more than half of the participants identified the following five issue areas as the common interests between the two nations. They are, in descending order, anti-terrorism, NPT (related to North Korea and Iran), trade, climate change, and financial stability. On the other end of the spectrum, respondents believed the two countries would not be able to see eye to eye on the issues of human rights and Taiwan, which shouldn't be surprising given what we have already found with respect to the challenges. In between were the issues of energy and Internet/cyber security, seen as common interests by almost one-third of the respondents.

Compared to the major challenges, Chinese IR scholars' perceptions of the common interests were more consistent across the four years of our surveys, especially the top and bottom issues. As we can see in Fig. 3.6 and

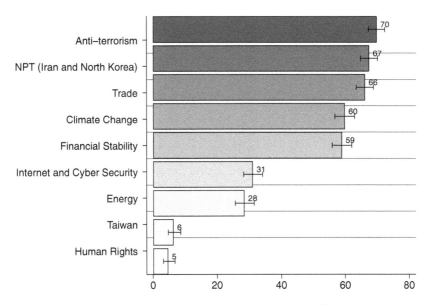

Fig. 3.5 Common interests in US–China relations. Note: The horizontal bars with 95% confidence intervals are percentages of respondents saying that the particular issue is a major challenge in US–China relations

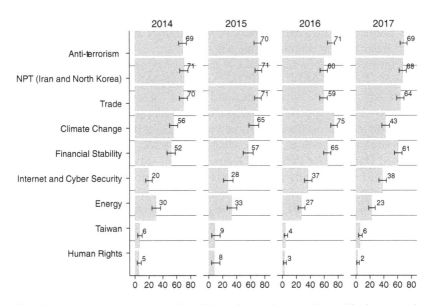

Fig. 3.6 Common interests in US–China relations by year. Note: The horizontal bars with 95% confidence intervals are percentages of respondents saying that the particular issue is a major challenge in US–China relations

Table 3.2   Ranking common interests in US–China relations by year

	2014	2015	2016	2017
Anti-terrorism	3	3	2	1
NPT (Iran and North Korea)	1	1	4	2
Trade	2	1	5	3
Climate change	4	4	1	5
Financial stability	5	5	3	4
Internet and cyber security	7	7	6	6
Energy	6	6	7	7
Taiwan	8	8	8	8
Human rights	9	9	9	9

Table 3.2, NPT, financial stability, and anti-terrorism were all perceived to be common interests for both countries across the years. The same can be said for the issues of Taiwan and human rights, neither of which received more than 10% of the responses.

Chinese participants perceive the trade issue as one top area of potential common interest; therefore, they hold a relatively benign or simplistic view on the trade imbalance between the United States and China. In their view, it is in both countries' interests to work together in order to address this problem. In other words, they may not have fully anticipated the Trump administration's coercive and punitive approach against China seen from the still ongoing trade war.

One interesting finding is on Chinese scholars' attitudes toward climate change. Between 2014 and 2016, more than half of the survey participants believed the United States and China could cooperate on climate change. The proportion of respondents picking climate change also increases steadily across these three years, peaking in 2016 at 75%. This is understandable because climate change was a top policy priority for the United States under President Obama, and our survey was implemented a few months after China and the United States signed the Paris Agreement on climate change.

However, in our 2017 survey, the proportion of participants who held this positive view on the climate change issue dropped precipitously to 43% ($p < 0.001$). This dramatic decline can be attributed to the Trump administration's antipathy toward climate change issues, culminating in the withdrawal of the United States from the Paris Agreement in June 2017. It is evident that our respondents quickly adjusted, comprehending that climate change would no longer be a viable area of cooperation between the United States and China.

US Intervention in China's Territorial Disputes

Due to its policy of rebalancing with respect to Asia and its security commitment to countries in the region, the United States is likely to intervene in the East and South China Seas disputes, especially in the event of conflicts between China and US allies, namely Japan and the Philippines. In this section, we evaluate whether US potential intervention is one of the reasons why the majority of Chinese IR scholars in our survey regarded China's territorial disputes in the East and South China Seas as the most challenging issues in the countries' bilateral relations.[11]

The Diaoyu/Senkaku disputes between China and Japan in the East China Sea have occupied the headlines since the collision incident in 2010 and further deteriorated after Japan's nationalization of the islands two years later. Since the United States is Japan's military ally in the region, the Chinese government has been deeply concerned over America's position in the dispute. In 2014, President Obama publicly stated that the dispute over the Diaoyu/Senkaku Islands is covered by the US–Japan security alliance treaty. It was the first time a US president had made such a claim, which intensified China's strategic apprehensions on the issue.

When asked about how likely it was that the United States would intervene in the Diaoyu/Senkaku dispute, around 70% of the participants thought US intervention was either likely or very likely if there were a military conflict between China and Japan (Fig. 3.7). This suggests that Chinese IR scholars do not hold unrealistic expectations regarding the strength of the US–Japan alliance and the role of Japan as the linchpin of American policies in the Asia-Pacific region. These perceptions persisted throughout the four-year period, which might also reflect a pragmatic approach on the Chinese government's part and explain China's efforts in recent years to alleviate the tension in the East China Sea.

Compared to the disputes over the Diaoyu/Senkaku Islands, Chinese IR scholars saw the United States as playing a lesser role in the South China Sea disputes. Over the four years, perceptions on the possibility of US involvement in these disputes was divided, with exactly half of the respondents believing the United States to be unlikely or very unlikely to intervene, and slightly less than half (49%) holding the opposite view (Fig. 3.8). A closer examination across the years, however, reveals that this

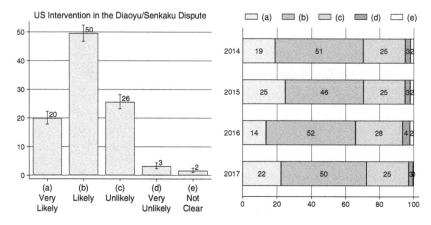

Fig. 3.7 US intervention in the Diaoyu/Senkaku dispute. Note: The left panel plots the distribution of the responses with 95% confidence intervals over the four-year period. The right panel plots the responses in each individual year of the survey. The numbers are in percentage points and may not add up to 100 due to rounding

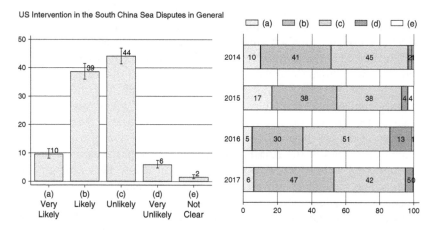

Fig. 3.8 US intervention in the South China Sea. Note: The left panel plots the distribution of the responses with 95% confidence intervals over the four-year period. The right panel plots the responses in each individual year of the survey. The numbers are in percentage points and may not add up to 100 due to rounding

overall split view is driven by results from 2016, where the proportion believing in US intervention dropped significantly to 35% ($p < 0.001$). The relatively optimistic view in 2016 on a possible US retreat from the South China Sea was short lived, probably the result of uncertainties surrounding the US presidential election.

Given that US intervention is perceived by Chinese IR scholars to be more likely in the East China Sea than the South China Sea, it may seem somewhat counterintuitive that fewer survey respondents considered the former to be a major challenge for US–China relations. Nevertheless, this seeming incoherence may be reconciled by an implicit understanding among the survey respondents that conflicts would be more likely to break out in the South China Sea. We will return to this point in Chap. 4 when we discuss China's bilateral relations with Japan and Southeast Asian states.

In sum, our four-year survey research reveals some interesting findings on Chinese IR scholars' perceptions of US–China relations. First, the CCPSIS participants showed a balanced view on US–China relations at the time as well as in the future. A majority of them believed that US–China relations were neither good nor bad in nature, with the rest slightly more optimistic than pessimistic. Second, the questions on specific issue areas suggest that scholars paid more attention to security-related issues, such as the Taiwan issue and the South China Sea disputes, than to economic or trade issues. On possible US involvement in China's territorial disputes, Chinese IR scholars worried more about America's role in the Diaoyu/Senkaku disputes than in the South China Sea. This shows that compared to US commitments to Southeast Asian states such as the Philippines, the US–Japan alliance is taken more seriously by Chinese scholars and possibly by the Chinese government as well.

SCHOLARLY DEBATES OVER SINO–AMERICAN RELATIONS

Are findings from our survey also reflected in the writings of Chinese IR scholars? In this section, we review the publications in the top five Chinese IR journals on the topic of US–China relations. Compared to the surveys, in which the majority of the respondents held a neutral view of these bilateral relations, there is a clearer division in the scholarly publications between the two major schools of thoughts in IR theory: the realists are more pessimistic and see more conflicts between the two countries, whereas liberals emphasize common interests and areas of cooperation.

Potential Conflicts and Increasing Pessimism

As early as 2013, the year before our first survey, many Chinese IR scholars were already suggesting in their published works that US–China competition would further intensify in the coming years.[12] Wang Zaibang, for example, argued that the next ten years would be a high-risk period for US–China relations, with more pressure from the United States' "rebalance to the Asia Pacific" and more areas of intensifying competition.[13] This pessimistic view on US–China relations increased dramatically in the following years. In 2015, Da Wei asserted that the strategic consensus between the United States and China had loosened and was almost on the verge of collapse, which could very well lead to a negative turn in their bilateral relations, beyond previously anticipated boundaries. He further warned that the US–China relationship was at a critical point and if not managed well, could escalate into a new Cold War.[14]

However, it is interesting to note that Chinese IR scholars have different views on why the two nations might head toward conflict. In particular, the articles we reviewed in the five leading Chinese IR journals point to at least three major reasons, all placing the blame on the United States. This is nevertheless consistent with the general consensus among Chinese IR scholars that China will not challenge the US and the international order, as we saw in the previous chapter.

The first reason is the so-called structural contradiction argument, which implicitly follows the logic of power transition theory in international relations as well as the Thucydides' Trap narrative. For example, Yuan Peng has argued that due to the narrowed power gap between the United States and China, the nature of their relationship has changed from "super versus normal" power to "the number one versus the number two." As China quickly closes the power gap against the United States, Washington has started to treat China as a "strategic competitor," which will inevitably lead to clashes between the United States and China in the military, geopolitical, and economic arenas.[15] In a similar vein, Mo Shengkai has stated that China's continuous rise in capabilities and America's general perception of its own decline have pushed US–China relations onto a more negative path.[16]

Second, many Chinese IR scholars singled out America's pivoting or rebalancing strategy as the major reason for increased bilateral tensions between the two countries. For example, Chu Shulong and Zhang Xiaoying argued that the United States has gradually changed its China policy from "engagement" to "restrainment" since Obama's second term. Although the United States has not moved to an overall containment strategy, its China policy features "partial containment" against China, especially in the South China Sea.[17] Wu Xinbo similarly concluded that the United States has adopted a mixed strategy toward China, with engagement, cooperation, restrainment, and balancing, which invariably has resulted in more tension and even confrontations between the two.[18] Xue Li further argued that Obama's "rebalancing" strategy actually was designed to compete with and even countervail the influence of China's Belt and Road Initiative (BRI).[19]

Third, some Chinese IR scholars have attributed the increasing tension and competition between the United States and China to the deficit of trust between political elites in both countries, echoing the main conclusion from an influential report penned by Kenneth Lieberthal and Wang Jisi, prominent scholars in the United States and China, respectively.[20] Wei Zhongyou and Huang Haitao, for example, highlighted the deepening political distrust between the two nations since the 2010s, which has led to more conflicting interests and has in the eyes of Chinese elites been further corroborated by policies such as US strategic deployment and adjustment in the Indo-Pacific region.[21] Much "credit" for this mutual distrust has been given to Trump, regarded by many scholars as the biggest variable in US–China relations.[22] For example, Wang Dong and Su Bingyan have argued that Trump's transactional approach to foreign policy could lead to short-term "turbulence" for US–China relations, and that Chinese policy makers should not engage in wishful thinking.[23]

With respect to the major challenges in US–China relations, similar to our survey findings, Chinese scholarly publications focused on Taiwan and the maritime disputes. For example, Liu Shilong argued that Taiwan will remain the most serious problem between the United States and China because it is part of the US containment strategy against China's rise.[24] Similarly, Hu Bo suggested that the focal points of US–China competition will be in Taiwan, the East China Sea, and the South China Sea, with the Taiwan issue listed as the number one flashpoint between the United States and China.[25] Other scholars warned that US involvement in the South China Sea has heightened the danger of confrontation between the United States and China, which may escalate and result in even more serious chain reactions than the Taiwan issue.[26]

Similar to what we found in the surveys, a smaller number of IR scholars discussed the danger of possible economic and trade disputes between the two nations. One of the earlier examples was Li Qingsi, who in 2013 gave a prescient warning that the economic complementarity between the two nations had decreased because of the countries' different economic developmental models, and consequently the possibility of trade disputes would increase significantly in the near future.[27] Similar voices began to hold more sway in the US election year, as scholars paid more attention in their writings to future trade disputes as a possible flashpoint between the two nations. Yu Xiang, for example, argued that despite achievements in trade, investment, and climate change cooperation during the Obama administration, troubles were brewing on a number of fronts, particularly in terms of bilateral trade.[28] Li Wei further pointed out that increasing trade frictions reflected broader competition between China and the US over power status, international public goods, and the establishment of free trade agreements.[29]

Scholars specializing in international political economy also highlighted possible tensions between the two nations in the financial domain. Li Wei, for example, argued that US–China competition might deteriorate in the currency and financial sectors, with the Chinese Yuan starting to challenge the US dollar's dominance in world economy after the 2008 global financial crisis.[30] Zhen Bingxi similarly postulated that institutional competition in global financial governance will become a new focal point in US–China relations.[31]

Common Interests and Fading Optimism

Conflicts and competition are not the only issues between the United States and China. As our survey research has already suggested, some scholars are more optimistic about the future of US–China relations.[32] While recognizing the potential for conflicts between the two nations, they place more emphasis on the countries' common interests, which could lead to more cooperation.[33] Consistent with our survey results, the common interests identified in the scholarly publications include nuclear non-proliferation in the Korean Peninsula, anti-terrorism in East Asia, Central Asia, and the Middle East, trade, and climate change. Some scholars were even confident that an adjusted cooperative framework built on these common interests could withstand the turbulences of the new Trump administration.[34] Others suggested that the two countries could find common ground in the Asia-Pacific region, given their shared interests in its economics and trade, regional multilateral cooperation, and security governance.[35]

For example, Xu Jian has argued that US–China relations will maintain some momentum, ensuring a bright future for cooperation and healthy competition. Although the two countries might experience some friction over trade, Xu feels this is only a minor aspect of their bilateral relations, whereas their economic interdependence will direct the long-term trends in US–China cooperation.[36] From a regional security perspective, Zhu Feng has argued that North Korean nuclear non-proliferation ranks high on the security threat agenda for both countries and thus is an area of potential collaboration.[37]

On global governance, Chinese scholars also believe that the United States and China share some common interests. For example, Da Wei argued that there are four pillars of US–China strategic interdependence: nuclear balance, economic interdependence, global climate change, and socio-economic linkages between the two nations.[38] Da emphasized the overarching threat from global climate change as a common interest between the two nations for future cooperation. In a similar vein, Zhao Xingzhu asserted that US–China cooperation in the climate change arena has gone beyond the domain of bilateral relations, with the two nations forging a "co-leadership" to foster international cooperation in global governance.[39]

Besides climate change, some Chinese scholars highlight the common interests between the two nations in the maritime domain. Wang Dong and Yang Yuchun argued that both countries wish to sustain the stability and order of the international sea lanes and thus have a shared incentive to work on a code of conduct to regulate their respective naval behaviors.[40] Zou Yanyan and Hou Yi further pointed out that the United States and China have in the past cooperated on many "non-sensitive" maritime issues, from fighting pirates to illegal fishing activities, and could continue to do so in the future.[41]

Nevertheless, such optimism about US–China relations has declined over time. This can best be seen in the number of articles on the "new type of major power relations" (NTMPR), which call for the two countries to set aside their differences and collaborate on issues of common interest.[42] Before 2016, 17 articles in the top five Chinese IR journals had NTMPR (the phrase or the acronym) in their titles, and most of them were optimistic. For example, Guo Zhenyuan argued that America's involvement in the Taiwan issue would decrease if an NTMPR between the two countries was successfully established. Jin Canrong and Wang Bo similarly suggested that the United States and China could cooperate in the military domain under the framework of an NTMPR.[43] In 2016, the number of such articles dropped to four, then to just one in the following year, suggesting that Chinese IR scholars have all but given up on the NTMPR idea since Trump became president in 2017.

CONCLUSION

Former Chinese ambassador to the United States Li Zhaoxing once commented retrospectively on his years of service that "US–China relations in the foreseeable future will not become better, nor will it become worse."[44] His view may represent the perspective of a seasoned diplomat, but it is also shared by Chinese IR scholars, the majority of whom in our four-year survey characterized US–China relations as "neither good nor bad" at the time as well as into the future. This finding is also echoed in the scholarly publications, though there is a clearer division between scholars who are optimistic that the two countries can establish a "new type of major power relations" and those who pessimistically believe that China's rise might trigger structural competition between the United States and China.

On more specific issues, both our survey research and our textual analyses of scholarly publications indicate that the biggest challenges in this bilateral relationship are Taiwan and the South China Sea disputes, while the two countries can cooperate on nuclear non-proliferation and anti-terrorism, based on their shared interests. Furthermore, we show that Chinese scholars are inclined to blame the United States—especially Obama's "pivot and rebalance" toward Asia as well as Trump's erratic leadership style—for the deterioration of relationship.

We also note two broader features in our findings. First, Chinese IR scholars take into account both historical patterns and current domestic political cycles within the United States when assessing the current status and future trajectory of US–China relations. We see this in their shifting opinions in the survey of 2016, the election year, and how some of them reverted to a more balanced view the following year. Second, Chinese IR scholars seem to be biased toward security issues in both their surveyed opinions and their scholarly writings. Indeed, the vast majority of the panels at the CCPSIS are related to security issues.[45]

Taken together, these two features may explain why many Chinese IR scholars and policy makers were taken aback by the rapid deterioration in bilateral relations, especially after Trump launched a trade war against China in 2018—most survey participants and publishing scholars had not considered trade disputes to be a major challenge between the two nations. It is unfair, however, to criticize Chinese IR scholars for not "predicting" the trade war. Truth be told, not many Americans predicted Trump's electoral victory or America's escalation of trade disputes with not only China but other countries as well, including some US allies.

Furthermore, as we saw in the 2017 survey, while still far behind the security issues, trade disputes were identified by nearly twice as many respondents as a major challenge in US–China relations. This is also reflected in the 2018 scholarly publications. Although Chinese IR scholars were still arguing that a new "Cold War" was not in the cards, they clearly had already realized that the stabilizing role of the countries' economic ties—the so-called cornerstone or stabilizer of bilateral relations—was diminishing under the Trump administration.[46] If we were to conduct a new survey today, the results would almost certainly paint a much gloomier picture of US–China relations.

NOTES

1. Huiyun Feng, "Foreign Policy Analysis in China," in Valerie Hudson and Klaus Brummer, eds. *Foreign Policy Analysis beyond North America* (Boulder: Lynne Rienner, 2015).
2. David Shambaugh, *Beautiful Imperialist: China Perceives America, 1972–1990* (Princeton: Princeton University Press, 1991); Wang Jianwei, *Limited Adversaries: Post-Cold War Sino-American Mutual Images* (Oxford: Oxford University Press, 2000); Michael Pillsbury, *China Debates the Future Security Environment* (Washington DC: National Defense University, 2000).
3. Andrew J. Nathan, "Authoritarian Resilience: Institutionalization and the Transition to China's Fourth Generation," in Christopher Marsh and June Teufel Dreyer, eds. *US–China Relations in the twenty-first Century* (Lanham: Lexington Books, 2003), 13–25; Andrew J. Nathan, "China's Changing of the Guard: Authoritarian Resilience," *Journal of Democracy* 14, no. 1 (2003): 6–17; Bruce Gilley, "The Limits of Authoritarian Resilience," *Journal of Democracy* 14, no. 1 (2003): 18–26.
4. Paul Krugman, "Taking on China," *New York Times*, March 14, 2010.

5. David M. Lampton, *Same Bed, Different Dreams: Managing US–China Relations, 1989–2000* (Berkeley: University of California Press, 2001).

6. Chris Isidore and Nicole Gaouette, "US Charges Chinese Hackers in Global Scheme Targeting Business and Military," CNN, 21 December 2018, available at: https://edition.cnn.com/2018/12/20/tech/chinese-hacker-charges/index.html; Joshua Berlinger, "European Union Diplomatic Cables Hack Linked to China, NYT Claims", CNN, 19 December 2018, available at: https://edition.cnn.com/2018/12/19/politics/european-union-hack-intl/index.html; David E. Sanger and Steven Lee Myers, "After a Hiatus, China Accelerates Cyberspying Efforts to Obtain US Technology," CNN, 29 November 2018, available at: https://www.nytimes.com/2018/11/29/us/politics/china-trump-cyberespionage.html.

7. Scott W. Harold, Martin C. Libicki, and Astrid Stuth Cevallos, *Getting to Yes with China in Cyberspace*, Research Report, RAND Corporation, Santa Monica, 2016, available at: https://www.rand.org/pubs/research_reports/RR1335.html. Also available in print form.

8. Ying Fu and Wu Shicun. "South China Sea: How We Got to This Stage," *The National Interest*, 9 May 2016, available at: https://nationalinterest.org/feature/south-china-sea-how-we-got-stage-16118.

9. Michael Yahuda, "China's New Assertiveness in the South China Sea," *Journal of Contemporary China* 22, no. 81 (2013): 446–459; Robert Ayson and Manjeet S. Pardesi, "Asia's Diplomacy of Violence: China–US Coercion and Regional Order," *Survival* 59, no. 2 (2017): 85–124.

10. Jethro Mullen, "Trump Attacks China on Trade but Misses the Mark," CNN, 5 December 2016, available at: https://money.cnn.com/2016/12/05/news/economy/trump-china-yuan-dollar-currency-taxes/index.html.

11. While we would like to include a similar question regarding Taiwan in the surveys, we were not able to do so due to the perceived sensitivity of the question.

12. Liu Jianhua, "Analysis on the Changes of US Asian Policy and Motivations—From a Long Term Perspective," *Journal of Contemporary Asia-Pacific Studies*, no. 3 (2013): 23–52. 刘建华: 《美国亚太政策的交替演变及其动因探析—基于长时段周期视角的考察》, 《当代亚太》 2013 年第 3 期, 第 23–52 页. ; Li Qingsi, "Foreign Policy Trends of Obama's Second Term and Discussions," *Contemporary International Relations*, no. 5 (2013): 24–29. 李庆四: 《奥巴马第二任期外交政策走势刍议》, 《现代国际关系》 2013 年第 5 期, 第 24–29 页.

13. Wang Zaibang, "China-US Relations into the High-Risk Period in the Next 10 Years, Three Indicators," *Contemporary International Relations*, no. 4 (2013): 13–15. 王在邦: 《中美关系十年后进入高风险期有三大指标性因素》, 《现代国际关系》 2013 年第 4 期, 第 13–15 页.

14. Da Wei, "Building China-US Relations' Long-Term Strategic Common Ground and Stable Framework," *Contemporary International Relations*, no. 6 (2015): 1–9. 达巍:《建立面向未来的中美关系战略共识与长期稳定框架》,《现代国际关系》2015 年第 6 期, 第 1–9 页.

15. Yuan Peng, "China's New Round of Reform and US–China's 'New Type of Major Power Relations'," *Contemporary International Relations*, no. 11 (2014): 1–9. 袁鹏:《中国新一轮改革与中美"新型大国关系"》,《现代国际关系》2014 年第 11 期, 第 1–9 页.

16. Mo Shengkai, "Power Shift and Preventive Cooperation," *World Economics and Politics*, no. 2 (2015): 16. 莫胜凯:《权力转移与预防性合作》,《世界经济与政治》2015 年第 2 期, 第 16 页.

17. Chu Shulong and Zhang Xiaoying, "Understanding and Making Judgement on Some Key Issues Related to the US," *Contemporary International Relations*, no. 7 (2016): 7–13. 楚树龙、章晓英:《对关于美国的几个重大问题的认识与判断》,《现代国际关系》2016 年第 7 期, 第 7–13 页.

18. Wu Xinbo, "China and US Relations Under the New Normal: Characters and Trends," *China International Studies*, no. 2 (2016): 14. 吴心伯:《新常态下中美关系发展的特征与趋势》,《国际问题研究》2016 年第 2 期, 第 14 页.

19. Xue Li, "US Rebalance Strategy and China's 'One Belt and One Road'," *World Economics and Politics*, no. 5 (2016): 56. 薛力:《美国再平衡战略与中国的"一带一路"》,《世界经济与政治》2016 年第 5 期, 第 56 页.

20. Kenneth Lieberthal and Wang Jisi, *Addressing US–China Strategic Distrust*, vol. 4 (Washington DC: Brookings, 2012).

21. Wei Zongyou, "US Strategic Adjustment in the Indo-Pacific and its Geostrategic Implications," *World Economics and Politics*, no. 10 (2013): 153–154. 韦宗友:《美国在印太地区的战略调整及其地缘战略影响》,《世界政治与经济》2013 年第 10 期, 第 153–154 页.; Huang Haitao, "Uncertainty, Risk Management, and Trust Decision Making—Observations on US–China Strategic Interactions," *World Economics and Politics*, no. 12 (2016): 129. 黄海涛:《不确定性、风险管理与信任决策—基于中美战略互动的考察》,《世界经济与政治》2016 年第 12 期, 第 129 页.

22. Ruan Zongze, "Trump's New Aspirations and China's Foreign Policy Choices," *China International Studies*, no. 2 (2017): 1–14. 阮宗泽:《特朗普"新愿景"与中国外交选择》,《国际问题研究》2017 年第 2 期, 第 1–14 页.; Wu Xinbo, "Trump and US–China Relations," *China International Studies*, no. 2 (2017): 15–28. 吴心伯:《特朗普执政与中美关系走向》,《国际问题研究》2017 年第 2 期, 第 15–28 页.

23. Wang Dong and Sun Bingyan, "Forward Looking at Trump's China Policy," *Contemporary International Relations*, no. 12 (2016): 15–23. 王

栋、孙冰岩: 《特朗普的对华政策前瞻》, 《现代国际关系》 2016 年第 12 期, 第 15–23 页.

24. Liu Shilong, "Japan-US Security Alliance and the Taiwan Issue," *Foreign Affairs Review*, no. 1 (2013): 110. 刘世龙: 《日美安全体系与台湾问题》, 《外交评论》 2013 年第 1 期, 第 110 页.

25. Hu Bo, "US–China Military Competition and Strategic Balance in the West Pacific," *World Economics and Politics*, no. 5 (2014): 64. 胡波: 《中美在西太平洋的军事竞争与战略平衡》, 《世界经济与政治》 2014 年第 5 期, 第 64 页.

26. Wang Weiguan and Chen Yao, "US Rebalance Strategy and its Impact on China's Maritime Disputes," *Contemporary Asia-Pacific Studies*, no. 1 (2016): 75–99. 王伟光、陈遥: 《美国"再平衡"战略对中国海上领土争端的影响》, 《当代亚太》 2016 年第 1 期, 第 75–99 页. ; Zhao Minghao, "US Policy Trend of Balancing China in the South China Sea," *Contemporary International Relations*, no. 1 (2016): 29–36. 赵明昊: 《美国在南海问题上对华制衡的政策动向》, 《现代国际关系》 2016 年第 1 期, 第 29–36 页. ; Wang Dong and Yang Yuchun, "China–US Relations in the Maritime Front: Challenges and Opportunities," *Contemporary International Relations*, no. 10 (2016): 47–49. 王栋、杨宇淳: 《海洋领域的中美关系: 挑战与机遇》, 《现代国际关系》 2016 年第 10 期, 第 47–49 页. ; Zou Yanyan and Hou Yi, "US–China Maritime Cooperation: Features and Directions in Moving Forward," *China International Studies*, no. 6 (2016): 18. 邹艳艳、侯毅: 《中美海洋合作: 特点与努力方向》, 《国际问题研究》 2016 年第 6 期, 第 18 页. Li Kaisheng, "Indirect Systemic Conflict—Potential Third Party Triggered US–China Conflict and Management," *World Economics and Politics*, no. 7 (2015): 90. 李开胜: 《间接性结构性冲突—第三方引发的中美冲突及其管控》, 《世界经济与政治》 2015 年第 7 期, 第 90 页.

27. Li Qingsi, "Analysing Foreign Policy Directions of Obama's Second Term." 李庆四: 《奥巴马第二任期外交政策走势刍议》, 《现代国际关系》 2013 年第 5 期, 第 24–29 页.

28. Yu Xiang, "Analysis of US–China Relations in the Obama Administration," *Contemporary International Relations,* no. 11 (2016): 40–47. 余翔: 《奥巴马任内中美经贸关系评述》, 《现代国际关系》 2016 年第 11 期, 第 40–47 页.

29. Li Wei, "Realist Institutionalism and US–China FTA Competition," *Journal of Contemporary Asia-Pacific Studies*, no. 3 (2016): 4–34. 李巍: 《现实制度主义与中美自贸区竞争》, 《当代亚太》 2016 年第 3 期, 第 4–34 页.

30. Li Wei, "The Rise of Financial Diplomacy in China," *World Economics and Politics*, no. 2 (2013): 86. 李巍: 《金融外交在中国的兴起》, 《世界经济与政治》 2013 年第 2 期, 第 86 页. ; Li Wei, "Institutional Competition

in US China Financial Diplomacy," *World Economics and Politics*, no. 4 (2016): 112. 李巍: 《中美金融外交中的国际制度竞争》，《世界经济与政治》2016 年第 4 期，第 112 页.

31. Zhen Bingxi, "New Trends and Future of US–China Economic and Trade Cooperation," *China International Studies,* no. 1 (2016): 77. 甄炳禧: 《中美经贸合作竞争新态势及前景》，《国际问题研究》2016 年第 1 期，第 77 页.

32. Dai Changzheng, "World Structure and Major Power Relations," *Contemporary International Relations*, no. 4 (2013): 6–9. 戴长征: 《当今世界格局与大国关系》，《现代国际关系》2013 年第 4 期，第 6–9 页.

33. Wang Lili, "Contemporary Chinese Public Diplomacy towards the US: Media Trend and Cognitive Space," *Contemporary International Relations*, no. 1 (2017): 45–51. 王莉丽: 《当前中国对美公共外交: 舆论态势与认知空间》，《现代国际关系》2017年第 1 期，第45–51页.

34. Wang Hao, "Analysis of Trump Government's Hook China Policy," *Journal of Contemporary Asia-Pacific Studies,* no 4 (2017): 65–85. 王浩: 《特朗普政府对华"挂钩"政策探析》，《当代亚太》2017 年第 4 期，第 65–85 页.; Song Guoyou, "Interests Shift, Changing Roles and Balance—US–China Relations under Trump," *Contemporary International Relations*, no. 8 (2017): 31–37. 宋国友: 《利益变化、角色转换和关系均衡—特朗普时期中美关系发展趋势》，《现代国际关系》2017 年第 8 期，第 31–37 页. Song was optimistic that Trump might speed up the process for a US–China balance.

35. Qi Huaigao, and Shi Yuanhua, "China's Peripheral Security Challenges and Big Neighborhood Diplomacy Strategy," *World Economics and Politics*, no. 6 (2013): 144–146. 祁怀高、石源华: 《中国的周边安全挑战与大周边外交战略》，《世界政治与经济》2013 年第 6 期，第 30–32 页.

36. Xu Jian, "Historical Conditions and Major Problems in Constructing a New Type of US–China Major Power Relations," *China International Studies*, no. 2 (2013): 8–19. 徐坚: 《构建中美新型大国关系的历史条件与主要问题》，《国际问题研究》2013 年第 2 期，第 8–19 页.

37. Zhu Feng pointed out that US and China can cooperate over the North Korean nuclear issue, and build a common recognition to settle the deadlock, see Zhu Feng "Trump's Coercive Diplomacy toward North Korea," *World Economics and Politics*, no. 6 (2017): 60–76. 朱锋: 《特朗普政府对朝鲜的强制外交》，《世界经济与政治》2017 年第 6 期，第 60–76 页.

38. Da Wei, "Path Choices for Constructing a US–China New Type of Major Power Relations," *World Economics and Politics*, no. 7 (2013): 62–64. 达巍: 《构建中美新型大国关系的路径选择》，《世界政治与经济》2013 年第 7 期，第 62–64 页.

39. Zhao Xingshu, "Analysing Cooperation between China and the US on the Climate Change Issue," *Contemporary International Relations*, no. 8

(2016): 47–56. 赵行姝: 《透视中美在气候变化问题上的合作》, 《现代国际关系》 2016 年第 8 期, 第 47–56 页.; Kang Xiao, "Multi-coexistence: Conceptual Reinvigoration of China and US Cooperation on Climate Change," *World Economics and Politics*, no. 7 (2016): 34.

40. Wang Chuanjian, "The South China Sea Issue and China-US Relations," *Journal of Contemporary Asia-Pacific Studies*, no. 2 (2014): 4–26. 王传剑: 《南海问题与中美关系》, 《当代亚太》 2014 年第 2 期, 第 4–26 页. Ma Rongjiu, "US–China Power Shift and Asian Regional Systems," *Journal of Contemporary Asia-Pacific Studies*, no. 1 (2014): 21–34. 马荣久: 《中美权力转移与亚洲地区体系》, 《当代亚太》 2014 年第 1 期, 第 21–34 页.

41. Zou Yanyan and Hou Yi, "China and US Maritime Cooperation: Features and Directions to Work Towards," *China International Studies*, no. 6 (2016): 18. 邹艳艳、侯毅: 《中美海洋合作: 特点与努力方向》, 《国际问题研究》 2016 年第 6 期, 第 18 页".

42. Wang Hao, "Constructing a New Type of Major Power Relations between China and the US: From Theoretical and Historical Comparative Perspectives," *Journal of Contemporary Asia-Pacific Studies*, no. 5 (2014): 51–75. 王浩: 《中美新型大国关系构建: 理论透视与历史比较》, 《当代亚太》 2014 年第 5 期, 第 51–75 页.

43. Jin Canrong and Wang Bo, "How to Build a New Type of Military Major Power Relations between the US and China," *Contemporary International Relations*, no. 3 (2015): 16–23 金灿荣、王博: 《如何构建中美新型大国军事关系》, 《现代国际关系》2015 年第 3 期, 第 16–23 页.

44. The comment was made in an address to the faculty and students of China Foreign Affairs University before he became the minister of Foreign Affairs in 2003.

45. Li Wei and Song Yiming, "The Miniature of China's International Relations Research."

46. Li Qingsi, "The Cause and Impact of Trump's Trade War with China," *Contemporary International Relations*, no. 6 (2018): 12–15. 李庆四: 《特朗普对华贸易战的原因及影响》, 《现代国际关系》 2018 年第 6 期, 第 12–15 页.

CHAPTER 4

On Chinese Foreign Policy and International Relations

In this chapter, we look at China's foreign policies more broadly through the eyes of Chinese international relations (IR) scholars. As in the previous chapters, our analyses draw on both our four-year survey data and textual analyses of publications in the top five Chinese IR journals. We focus on two key domains of China's foreign policies. First, we examine how Chinese scholars perceive China's foreign policy orientation and key principles in foreign policy as well as its policy changes. Second, we explore Chinese scholars' perceptions of China's relations with major powers and regions in the world, except for the United States, which we have discussed in the previous chapter.

There are three sections in this chapter. First, we discuss our findings from our four-year survey research. Although most participants have expressed a positive attitude toward China's foreign policy, they believe that China needs to change some foreign policy principles and practices, such as its keeping-a-low-profile principle, non-alliance policy, and policy toward North Korea. In the second section, we report findings from our textual analyses of articles in the top five Chinese IR journals, highlighting the similarities and differences between the survey results and the scholarly publications. In the conclusion, we discuss the implications of our findings for studying China's foreign policy.

© The Author(s) 2019
H. Feng et al., *How China Sees the World*,
https://doi.org/10.1007/978-981-15-0482-2_4

Surveying China's Foreign Policy

On China's Foreign Policy and Principles

In our four-year surveys, we asked participants whether or not they considered China's overall foreign policies to be "very strong," "strong with restraint," "weak," or "very weak"; alternatively, they could say they were "not clear." We can see from Fig. 4.1 that the surveyed Chinese Community of Political Science and International Studies (CCPSIS) participants predominantly believed Chinese foreign policy to be strong with restraint (62%), while about a third (29%) said that it was weak. In contrast, the two more extreme views received little support, with only 4% and 2% of the respondents considering Chinese foreign policy to be "very strong" or "very weak," respectively. These results suggest that the majority of Chinese IR scholars are satisfied with the general direction of the country's foreign policies, which they believe to be strong but not to the point of threatening; this is consistent with the finding in Chap. 2 that China is not perceived to be challenging the existing world order. Comparing the responses to this question over time, we further note a significant increase in 2017 in the number of respondents who saw Chinese foreign policy as

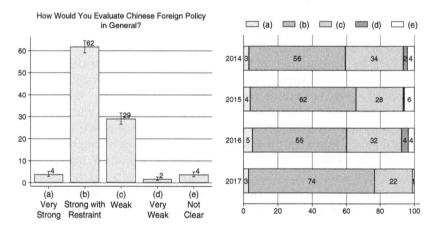

Fig. 4.1 Evaluation of Chinese foreign policy in general. Note: The left panel plots the distribution of the responses with 95% confidence intervals over the four-year period. The right panel plots the responses in each individual year of the survey. The numbers are in percentage points and may not add up to 100 due to rounding

very strong or strong with restraint (77%), more than in any of the previous three years ($p < 0.01$). This growing level of confidence is once again consistent with our findings in Chap. 2 about China's rising power.

Chinese foreign policy has been widely portrayed in both popular media and academic writings as undergoing an "assertive turn" since the 2008 global financial crisis.[1] Our surveys show that Chinese IR scholars seem to share the same view. Figure 4.2 plots the responses from our four-year surveys to the question on whether or not they agree that China's foreign policy has become more assertive since the 2008 global financial crisis. Across the four survey years, 74% of the respondents agreed (62% with reservations) that Chinese foreign policy has become more assertive since 2008. This result is consistent with the earlier discussion on Chinese foreign policy in general, which also reflects Chinese scholars' increasing confidence in Chinese foreign policy. Examining the responses over time reveals some changes in 2016, when more participants (29%) disagreed with the statement compared to the other three years ($p < 0.001$). This shift in opinion may be a result of China's foreign policy challenges that year, as we discussed in earlier chapters, including the Hague ruling that denied China's historic claims in the South China Sea.

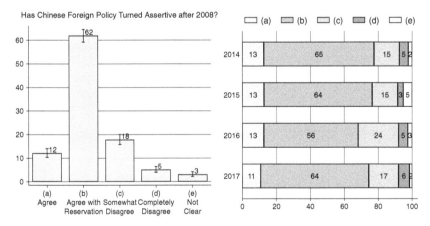

Fig. 4.2 Views on the assertiveness of China's foreign policy (%). Note: The left panel plots the distribution of the responses with 95% confidence intervals over the four-year period. The right panel plots the responses in each individual year of the survey. The numbers are in percentage points and may not add up to 100 due to rounding

When Deng Xiaoping started economic reform and opening-up in China in 1979, he publicly set a foreign policy principle of "keeping a low profile" (韬光养晦, *Taoguang Yanghui*, often referred to as TGYH), which became the country's guiding principle in the subsequent three decades. Along with TGYH, China officially follows a "non-alliance" policy, and frequently criticizes military alliances as "Cold War relics" unconducive to regional stability and peace. Some scholars have argued that China's assertive turn in foreign policy indicates a fundamental shift in these long-held principles.[2] There have also been internal debates regarding whether China should abandon or at least adjust these principles.[3] One prominent proponent of the latter is Yan Xuetong, who wrote in 2010 that "what China faces today is not only the problem of adjusting foreign policy strategies, but also that of adjusting foreign policy principles, namely whether to adjust the principles of *Taoguang Yanghui* and non-alignment."[4]

Chinese IR scholars in our survey appear to hold a similar view. Figure 4.3 shows the responses to the question, "Should the Chinese foreign policy principle of TGYH be changed?" Across the three years when the question was asked, a majority of the respondents either fully

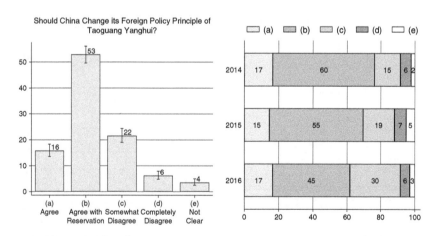

Fig. 4.3 China's foreign policy principle of *Taoguang Yanghui* (TGYH). Note: The left panel plots the distribution of the responses with 95% confidence intervals over the four-year period. The right panel plots the responses in each individual year of the survey. The numbers are in percentage points and may not add up to 100 due to rounding

agreed (16%) or agreed with reservation (53%) that China should change this principle. There was a downward trend (Fig. 4.3), however, as the proportion of respondents in support of change dropped from 77% in 2014 to 70% in 2015 ($p < 0.05$) and 62% in 2016 ($p < 0.05$). Conversely, the percentage of opposing respondents ballooned, increasing from 21% in 2014 to 36% in 2016. As mentioned, China had diplomatic setbacks that year, which could have encouraged more participants to rethink the wisdom of adjusting the TGYH approach.

We also asked respondents whether or not they think China "should form military alliances with other countries." The implicit country of choice is Russia—the most likely candidate should China form such an alliance. As can be seen in Fig. 4.4, here the results are more divided. Across the four survey years, slightly more than half (53%) of the respondents agreed that China should change its non-alliance strategy, while slightly less than half (45%) disagreed. Similar to the findings on TGYH, there was a declining level of support for military alliances over time. In 2014, three-fifths of the survey participants believed that China should change its "non-alliance" principle. This proportion dropped to 54% in 2015 ($p < 0.05$) and further dipped below 50% in 2016 ($p < 0.05$) before reaching 49% in 2017.

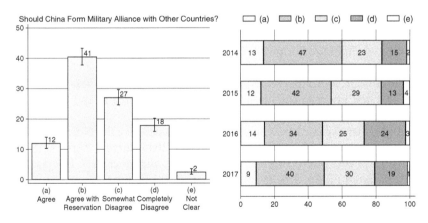

Fig. 4.4 China and military alliance. Note: The left panel plots the distribution of the responses with 95% confidence intervals over the four-year period. The right panel plots the responses in each individual year of the survey. The numbers are in percentage points and may not add up to 100 due to rounding

While these changes can certainly be attributed to China's diplomatic setbacks in 2016, one would expect those to have intensified the belief that China should reverse its non-alignment strategy and seek support from countries such as Russia to offset the United States' security alliance network in the Asia-Pacific region. Our seemingly contradictory finding may be explained by China having a range of alternative strategies between the two extreme options of military alliances or non-alliance, such as quasi-alliances, coalitions, and strategic partnerships, the last of which has gained much more in popularity lately. In other words, the reduced support for military alliances that we found does not necessarily mean that Chinese IR scholars wish to stick with the original "non-alliance" approach. We will return to this point in the textual analyses below to uncover in scholarly writings more nuanced positions on the non-alliance principle.

For China, the Sino–North Korean Mutual Aid and Cooperation Friendship Treaty signed in 1961 and remaining in effect today is perhaps the closest equivalent to a military alliance, as it stipulates that each of the signatories should undertake all measures necessary to oppose any foreign aggression against the other. During the course of the four-year survey period, however, North Korea has increasingly become a liability in China's foreign policy, especially since Pyongyang under Kim Jung-un has since 2013 increased its provocative activities through a series of nuclear and missile tests on the Korean Peninsula. To capture this sentiment, in our surveys, we asked participants whether or not China should change its policy toward North Korea. The results, displayed in Fig. 4.5, show that an overwhelming majority (80%) of the respondents was not happy with the current policy, and such dissatisfaction remained stable throughout the four years, indicating widespread frustration among Chinese IR scholars over the government's policy toward North Korea in the escalating nuclear crisis.

To further explore how Chinese IR scholars perceive the North Korean crisis, we asked a follow-up question in the 2017 survey: "Are the Six-Party Talks key to resolving the North Korean nuclear crisis?" The results are presented in Fig. 4.6. It appears that the participants on average did not put much faith in the prospect of the Six-Party Talks—60% of them somewhat or completely disagreed that the talks were key to resolving the crisis. This pessimistic view also departs from that of the Chinese government, which continues to insist on getting the six countries back to the negotiation table.

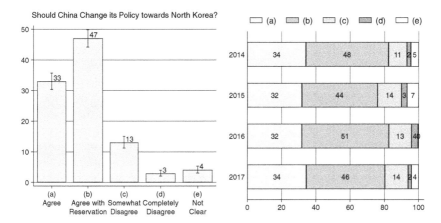

Fig. 4.5 China's policy towards North Korea. Note: The left panel plots the distribution of the responses with 95% confidence intervals over the four-year period. The right panel plots the responses in each individual year of the survey. The numbers are in percentage points and may not add up to 100 due to rounding

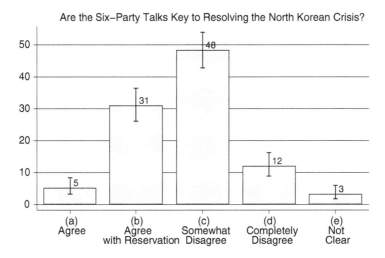

Fig. 4.6 Attitude on the future of the Six-Party Talks (%). Note: The bars represent the proportion of responses with 95% confidence intervals

In short, Chinese IR scholars in our four-year survey show relatively strong confidence in and satisfaction with China's foreign policy. They are not shy about admitting that Chinese foreign policy has taken a relatively assertive direction after the global financial crisis. This view is backed by the prevailing opinion that China should change its long-held TGYH foreign policy principle. However, they are divided on the question of whether or not China should pursue military alliances and in doing so, reverse its non-alliance policy. Furthermore, the majority of the surveyed participants believed that China should change its North Korea policy and that the Six-Party Talks will not be efficient or useful in defusing the North Korean nuclear crisis—which notably was identified as one of the top issues of common interest between China and the United States, as we saw in Chap. 3. The finding regarding North Korea is somewhat surprising, as it is not consistent with the official stance of the Chinese government, which emphasizes the historical ties between the two nations. This rather unexpected result serves as a reminder that Chinese IR scholars do not necessarily agree with Beijing's foreign policies, though it has yet to be seen whether such disagreement can eventually translate into policy changes.

China's Bilateral Relations with Other Countries

In Chap. 3, we discussed how Chinese IR scholars perceive the country's bilateral relations with the United States. In the surveys, we further asked participants to evaluate China's relations with other countries or country blocs, such as Russia, Japan, India, the Association of Southeast Asian Nations (ASEAN), the European Union (EU), Latin American countries, and African countries. These questions and answer choices were worded similarly to the question on China–US relations, though we only asked for an evaluation of the current relationship.

We start by looking at China's relations with its immediate neighbors. Figure 4.7 shows Chinese participants' perceptions of China–Russia relations in the four-year surveys. Overall, an overwhelming majority of participants (85%) believed China–Russia relations to be "very good" or "good." Furthermore, none of the 1200-plus respondents across the four years described the relationship as "antagonistic" (consequently, that category is not shown in Fig. 4.7). This is hardly surprising. As mentioned before, the common threats and pressures from the West in general and the United States in particular have pushed China and Russia closer in the

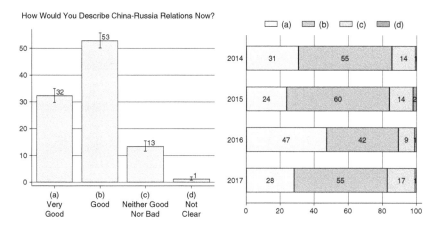

Fig. 4.7 China–Russia relations. Note: The left panel plots the distribution of the responses with 95% confidence intervals over the four-year period. The right panel plots the responses in each individual year of the survey. The numbers are in percentage points and may not add up to 100 due to rounding

2010s. Both countries have been consistently improving their strategic partnership with frequent high-level visits, joint military exercises, and energy cooperation, exemplified by the two governments signing a 30-year, $400 billion gas deal in 2014.[5]

As we've seen multiple times by now, there was a jump in 2016, with the proportion of positive perceptions of China–Russia relations rising. In particular, almost half of the participants perceived the bilateral relationship as "very good" (47%), significantly more than in the other three years ($p < 0.001$). Recalling our previous discussions on China's diplomatic challenges in 2016, it is not difficult to understand the significant "warming" in China's relationship with Russia that year. This positive shift was short-lived, however, as the responses in 2017 reverted to 2014 and 2015 levels.

In view of China's relationship with Japan, another important neighbor, Chinese IR scholars are markedly less sanguine. As can be seen in Fig. 4.8, 37% of the respondents regarded the two countries as in an antagonistic relationship, and only two respondents in the entire sample used "very good" to describe Sino–Japanese relations. That said, half of the respondents considered the relationship to be neither good nor bad, which is surprising given their bitter history in the early twentieth century and the ongoing territorial disputes over the Diaoyu/Senkaku islands in

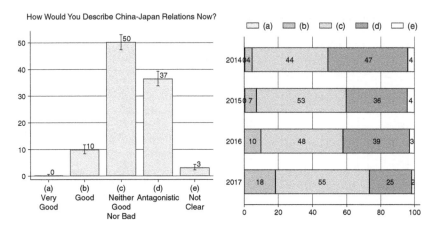

How Would You Describe China-Japan Relations Now?

Fig. 4.8 China–Japan relations. Note: The left panel plots the distribution of the responses with 95% confidence intervals over the four-year period. The right panel plots the responses in each individual year of the survey. The numbers are in percentage points and may not add up to 100 due to rounding

the East China Sea. In the latter case, a series of events occurred in the early 2010s that heavily strained bilateral relations. In 2010, the "trawler collision" crisis led to a diplomatic standoff between China and Japan for more than two weeks. In 2012, the Japanese government nationalized three of the Diaoyu/Senkaku Islands, triggering a new round of diplomatic crises between the two nations. Since then, China has started to regularly dispatch government vessels and airplanes to patrol the Diaoyu/Senkaku area in order to affirm its sovereign claims over the disputed islands. In response, Japan has sent its coast guard vessels to the same area to defend its claims.[6]

These tensions evidently contributed to an overly negative view of Sino–Japanese relations in the 2014 survey—almost half (47%) of the surveyed conference participants believed China and Japan to be adversaries. However, if we examine the four-year trend, it is clear that Chinese scholars have gradually revised their views in a more positive direction. In 2014, only 4% of the respondents perceived the bilateral relations to be "good." But this number more than quadrupled to 18% in 2017. During the same period, the number of pessimists continued to decline, dropping to 36% in 2015 ($p < 0.01$), rising slightly to 39% in 2016, and settling at 25% in 2017 ($p < 0.001$). However, given the troubled history between the two nations in the early 2010s, the relatively neutral perception from Chinese

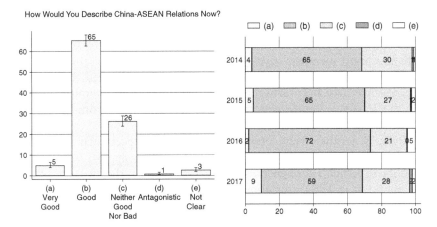

Fig. 4.9   China–ASEAN relations. Note: The left panel plots the distribution of the responses with 95% confidence intervals over the four-year period. The right panel plots the responses in each individual year of the survey. The numbers are in percentage points and may not add up to 100 due to rounding

IR scholars should be interpreted as a somewhat optimistic view of China–Japan relations and is consistent with the findings regarding the Diaoyu/Senkaku Islands described in Chap. 3.

Even though China has maritime disputes with some ASEAN countries in the South China Sea, our surveys show that 70% of the participants across the four years perceived China–ASEAN relations to be "very good" or "good" (Fig. 4.9). Most of the rest held a neutral view, choosing "neither good nor bad" (26%). These views were quite stable over time, as the distributions of the responses in three of the four years were nearly identical. The exception is 2016, when the perception of the relationship between China and ASEAN was even more positive ($p < 0.01$), despite some of the diplomatic setbacks in the South China Sea discussed earlier.

The largely positive evaluation of China–ASEAN relations can be attributed to ASEAN members' divided positions on China's increased presence in the South China Sea. While members such as Vietnam and the Philippines wanted ASEAN countries to stand up against Chinese pressure, other members such as Cambodia, with significant economic ties to China, were wary of angering Beijing. There was no mention of the Hague case in the ASEAN chairman's statement in 2016, for example, exposing the deep division within ASEAN on the South China Sea disputes.

Furthermore, although the United States actively encouraged ASEAN to stand by its side in challenging China's extensive claims in the South China Sea, through frequent FONOP (Freedom of Navigation Operation) activities, most members have chosen not to take sides, thereby avoiding becoming entangled in the US–China competition.[7] Instead, China and the ASEAN have been actively negotiating a "code of conduct" in the South China Sea, signifying goodwill and common effort from both sides in managing the disputes.

India is another rising power in Asia, with a spectacular economic growth rate in recent years. The China–India relationship has long been a priority in China's foreign policy, not least because the two neighbors fought a war in 1962 over disputed territories along the border, some of which remain unsettled. In our survey, slightly more than half of the participants (53%) viewed China–India relations as "neither good nor bad" across the four years (Fig. 4.10). The rest of the respondents were more positive than negative, with over three times more deeming the relationship to be "good" or "very good" (37%) than "antagonistic" (8%).

These optimistic evaluations reflect a warming in bilateral relations after Narendra Modi came to power in 2014 and adopted an active "Act East Policy" to strengthen India's relations with East Asian and Southeast

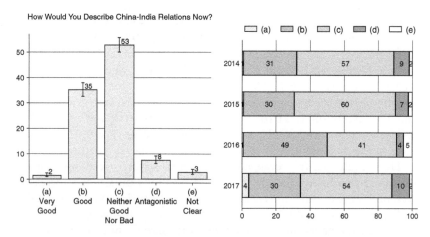

Fig. 4.10 China–India relations. Note: The left panel plots the distribution of the responses with 95% confidence intervals over the four-year period. The right panel plots the responses in each individual year of the survey. The numbers are in percentage points and may not add up to 100 due to rounding

Asian countries, including China. In the same year, Chinese president Xi Jinping made his first official visit to India, which was reciprocated by Modi a year later. Both leaders agreed that the two countries should strengthen cooperation through various multilateral platforms, including the BRICS (Brazil, Russia, India, China and South Africa) international forum, the Shanghai Cooperation Organization (SCO), and the Group of 20.

Between 2015 and 2016, China and India launched several new mechanisms for cooperation. For example, in November 2015, the first dialogue between the Development Research Center of the State Council of China and the National Institution for Transforming India (NITI Aayog) was held in Beijing, with officials from both countries discussing issues of common interest, such as structural reform, the global economic situation, and China–India economic cooperation. In February 2016, China and India held the first round of a maritime cooperation dialogue, at the end of which the two sides agreed to expand cooperation in marine science and technology, naval exchanges, fisheries, shipping, and other related areas. These positive developments likely contributed to a surge of optimism in the 2016 survey, when the proportion of participants perceiving the bilateral relations as "good" increased dramatically from 30% in the previous two years to 49% ($p < 0.001$).

This upward trend was bucked in 2017, however, with the proportion of participants considering China–India relations to be "good" or "very good" significantly dropping from 49% to 34% and the proportion of negative responses more than doubling. This dramatic shift is understandable, though. At the time of our survey, the two countries were locked in a military standoff in Doklam after China constructed a road near a tri-junction border area between India, China, and Bhutan. In fact, the positive responses could have slid further if our survey had been implemented a few weeks later, when tensions escalated into a physical brawl involving soldiers from the two sides kicking, punching, and throwing stones at each other at the border.[8]

In addition to these close neighbors, we also asked respondents to evaluate China's relations with three regions—Europe, Africa, and Latin America—that are geographically further away but have become increasingly important for Beijing as its economy expands. The EU has been China's largest trading partner since 2003, with bilateral trade exceeding $600 billion in 2014, and is an important source of and destination for investments, with Chinese investments in Europe exceeding European investments in China for the first time in 2014.[9] In 2000, when the first Forum of China Africa Cooperation was launched in 2000, bilateral trade between China and Africa reached $10 billion, and by 2013, the volume had risen to $200 billion, making China Africa's largest trading partner since 2009.[10] Similarly, Chinese trade with Latin America grew at an annual rate of 27% between 2000 and 2013, more than twice the average growth rate of Latin America's other foreign trade during the same period. By 2017, China had become the second-largest trading partner of Latin America after the United States, and Latin America was the second-largest destination for Chinese foreign investment, after Asia.[11]

Considering the flourishing economic ties and the lack of major disputes, it should be hardly surprising that the survey participants were overwhelmingly positive regarding China's relations with these regions. Africa in particular was viewed as having the best relationship with China. Nearly nine out of ten respondents (87%) deemed bilateral relation to be either "very good" or "good" across the four years (Fig. 4.11). Latin America and the EU were neck and neck, with 69% and 71% of the respondents considering their respective relations with China to be "very good" or "good" (Fig. 4.12). These views were also quite stable over time (Fig. 4.13). The only exception was Latin America in 2016, when there

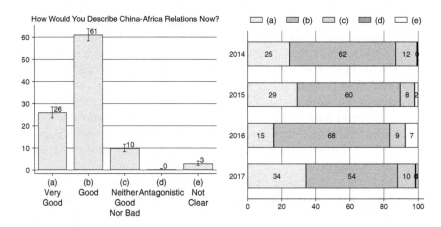

Fig. 4.11 China–Africa relations. Note: The left panel plots the distribution of the responses with 95% confidence intervals over the four-year period. The right panel plots the responses in each individual year of the survey. The numbers are in percentage points and may not add up to 100 due to rounding

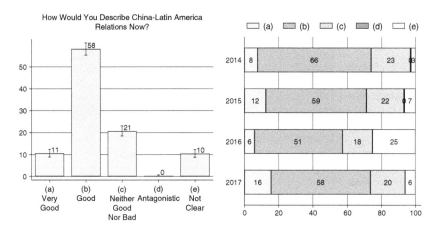

Fig. 4.12 China–Latin America relations. Note: The left panel plots the distribution of the responses with 95% confidence intervals over the four-year period. The right panel plots the responses in each individual year of the survey. The numbers are in percentage points and may not add up to 100 due to rounding

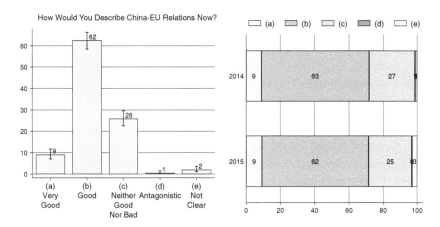

Fig. 4.13 China–EU relations. Note: The left panel plots the distribution of the responses with 95% confidence intervals over the four-year period. The right panel plots the responses in each individual year of the survey. The numbers are in percentage points and may not add up to 100 due to rounding

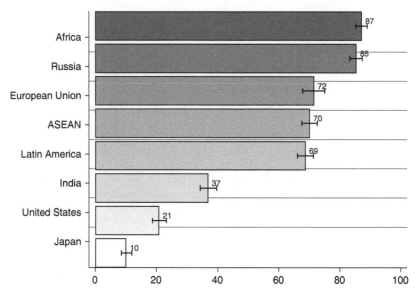

Fig. 4.14 Ranking China's bilateral relations. Note: The horizontal bars with 95% confidence intervals are percentages of respondents saying that China's relationship with the particular country or country bloc is good or very good, averaged over the four survey years. The responses for the EU are averaged over the two survey years in which the question was asked

was a substantial uptick in the responses of "not clear" ($p < 0.01$). The increased sense of uncertainty was likely the result of major political changes in three important countries in the region—Argentina, where the conservative opposition candidate, Mauricio Macri, won the presidential election in November 2015; Venezuela, where the United Socialist Party of Venezuela lost control of the assembly in December 2015; and Brazil, where President Dilma Rousseff was impeached in April 2016.

Putting everything together, we can rank the seven bilateral relationships discussed above as well as Sino–US relations, addressed in the previous chapter, according to the average proportions of respondents who viewed China's relations with them to be good or very good. It is clear from Figs. 4.14 and 4.15 that according to Chinese IR scholars, China has maintained warm and steady relationships with Africa, Russia, the EU, ASEAN, and Latin America, but cooler and volatile relationships with the United States, India, and Japan. Consistent with our findings in Chap. 3

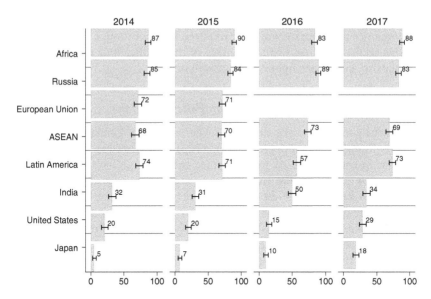

Fig. 4.15 China's bilateral relations by year. Note: The horizontal bars with 95% confidence intervals are percentages of respondents saying that China's relationship with the particular country or country bloc is good or very good. There were no responses for the EU in 2016 and 2017 when the question was not asked

regarding the challenges and common interests in Sino–US relations, where respondents placed more emphasis on security than economic issues, here it appears that security concerns similarly have a much bigger impact in shaping Chinese IR scholars' perceptions of the outside world.

SCHOLARLY WRITINGS ON CHINA'S FOREIGN POLICY AND BILATERAL RELATIONS

The surveys provide us with an overall picture of Chinese IR scholars' views on Chinese foreign policy and bilateral relations. Due to the space limitations of our questionnaires, however, we did not follow up with "how" and "why" questions and consequently were unable to capture more nuanced arguments. For example, as we mentioned earlier, scholars may not embrace the idea of China entering a full military alliance but instead may support some alternative arrangement, such as a strategic partnership, which could still be interpreted as a partial departure from the non-alliance principle. But in the survey, these scholars did not have the opportunity to elaborate and were required to dichotomize their answers. In this section, we use textual analyses of the publications of Chinese IR scholars to shed more light on this possibility.

On China's Foreign Policy Principles

We start by looking at the debate on whether or not China should abandon its foreign policy principle of TGYH, a topic that has become quite popular in the top five IR journals since the 2008 global financial crisis. Our review suggests that the majority of scholars insist TGYH should remain the key principle directing Chinese foreign policy. The common justification they offer is that even though China has risen to become a major economic power, it is still facing many domestic challenges—including resource shortages, environmental degradation, and financial instability—that could threaten its long-term growth. Therefore, China should continue to uphold TGYH and focus on economic development. Some realists, such as Zhang Ruizhuang, even assert that China is only just turning from a weak power into a strong power, so it should place *more* emphasis on TGYH in this transitional phase.[12] Similarly, Liu Jianhua argues that China will face increasing pressure from America's "pivot" or "rebalancing" policy in the Asia-Pacific region. Therefore, China should maintain TGYH and strategically "fight against the United States without damaging the overall relationship with the US" (斗而不破).[13]

That a majority of the writers in these Chinese scholarly publications argue for retaining TGYH seems to contradict the survey findings, in which more than half of the scholars advocated for change. The most likely explanation is that the survey question forced respondents to pick one of the two somewhat extreme options, while in reality their views could have been more nuanced. Indeed, many scholars, including the ones cited above, argue that while China should stick to TGYH, some adjustments are needed to reflect the changing international environment. In particular, they point out that Deng Xiaoping's original speech on the principle of TGYH also contained the phrase *"you suo zuo wei"* (YSZW), or "striving for achievement."[14] In this vein, they assert that given China's increased economic and political power, the time has come for China to take up some responsibilities in addition to reassuring other countries with its peaceful development strategy.[15] Similarly, Wu Zhicheng points out that on the basis of clearly defined Chinese national interests, China should revise its old strategic indecisiveness, passive measures, and sit-and-wait approach for opportunities and instead proactively strive for more achievements in foreign policy.[16] Other scholars, such as He Lan, are more cautious, proposing that TGYH and YSZW should be balanced and systemically managed to avoid the dangers arising from overemphasizing the G2, or from such narratives as the Chinese Century and the China Model.[17]

Similar to the findings on TGYH, most articles on China's non-alliance principle advocate that China should stick with it. For example, Chen Zhimin points out that non-alliance is a fundamental principle of China's foreign policy and contends that no change is needed.[18] In addition, Liu Bowen and Fang Changping argue that China can build a "neighborhood friendship network" (周边伙伴关系网络) and establish an open, multilateral, and multi-layered system of bilateral relations that are different from military alliances and tributary systems. China therefore should send its neighbors a clear signal regarding its non-alliance principle.[19]

While they are a minority, some scholars implicitly challenge this "non-alliance" doctrine. For example, in evaluating China's security cooperation with Russia, Wang Shuchun and Wan Qingsong argue that in the long term, China and Russia should not rule out the possibility of upgrading their current strategic cooperation to a formal military alliance. In a similar vein, Ling Shengli argues that China's current non-alliance policy is based on China's national interests. Whether China will change this policy depends mainly on an overall recalibration of China's changing national interests. In other words, if China's future national interests need a military alliance, then this principle can be changed.[20]

Recall that in our surveys, more than half of the participants agreed that China should change its non-alliance principle. One possible explanation for this discrepancy between our survey research and textual analyses of scholarly publications is that Chinese scholars are hesitant to openly challenge the official line of China's foreign policy doctrines, such as the principle of non-alliance. A more plausible explanation, as we suggested above, is that scholars were not able to offer a more nuanced answer in response to the survey question. Indeed, a number of authors have advocated that China should modify its "non-interference" policy. For example, Zhen Ni and Chen Zhimin argue that although China should stay faithful to the principle of non-interference with respect to internal affairs, it should adopt a more flexible approach in foreign policy practices. In particular, when China votes as a member of the UN Security Council, it has to balance two prevailing normative principles: non-interference on the one hand and the responsibility to protect on the other.[21] Similarly, Zhang Qi argues that China should consider how to increase its diplomatic involvement in international humanitarian interventions sanctioned by the United Nations.[22] Li Yongzhen further points out that China has already modified its non-interference principle in foreign policy by proposing a new "consultative involvement" approach as a "Chinese wisdom or Chinese solution" to global governance, which is based on its own domestic consultative political practices.[23]

In our surveys, an overwhelming majority of participants believed that China should change its policy toward North Korea. In the scholarly publications, however, we do not see many scholars advocating for such change. Most articles related to North Korea simply elaborate upon and justify China's official policies, such as the principle of non-nuclearization on the Korean Peninsula, the dual-track negotiation approach, and the search for a peaceful resolution through the Six-Party Talks.[24] One notable exception is Jia Qingguo, who claims that the historical foundation of the China–Korea relationship has changed, and it is therefore imperative for the Chinese government to re-evaluate its policy toward North Korea and restore a "*normal* bilateral relation" with Pyongyang.[25] Jia's argument actually triggered a serious debate in the Chinese media in late 2017, in which he was criticized by scholars who support China's traditional friendship with North Korea.

Some observers regarded this public debate as a signal that China will indeed change its policy toward North Korea.[26] Nonetheless, despite the issuance of some unusually strong statements from Beijing, admonishing Kim's nuclear tests, it remained "business as usual." As a matter of fact, instead of alienating and punishing North Korea, as Jia proposed, China further strengthened its bilateral ties with North Korea after several summit meetings between Xi and Kim in 2018 and 2019. Unfortunately, our survey research ended in 2017. Otherwise, it would have been interesting to examine how Chinese participants viewed China's policy change toward North Korea in 2018, something that deserves more serious inquiry from both academic scholars and policy analysts studying Chinese foreign policy in the future.

On China's Bilateral Relations

Similar to our survey findings, most of the relevant articles in the Chinese scholarly publications have highlighted the strategic partnership between

China and Russia. In their writings, the majority of the scholars stress that China and Russia share a common threat perception with respect to the United States. Strategically speaking, China and Russia need each other for strategic and political support. These writers also echo the official narrative that the bilateral relationship between China and Russia remains the best in China's history. Nevertheless, some are cautioning against potential pitfalls in the future relationship between the two nations. As one scholar puts it, although Sino–Russian relations are at their best, the imbalance in economic relations between the two countries may lead to an erosion of political trust, which could negatively affect the relationship.[27] Similarly, Shi Ze cautions that the strategic relationship between Russia and China does not have a solid foundation on which to build economic cooperation.[28] From a strategic perspective, Wang Shuchun and Liu Sisi argue that Russia's "new Asia strategy" aims to increase its influence and power in Asia, which could trigger a competition between China and Russia.[29]

On China's relations with Japan, there is a general sense of pessimism in the published articles. Chinese scholars list three main reasons for a troubled relationship between the two nations. First, China's rise has deepened Japan's strategic suspicions and apprehensions. China's GDP surpassed Japan's in 2010, making it the second-largest economy in the world. It seems inevitable that there will be structural competition between China and Japan in the international system. Li Xiangyang, for example, argues that it is difficult to restore Sino–Japanese relations to the status prior to the Diaoyu/Senkaku disputes in 2012. Structural competition and conflict will become a new normal for China–Japan relations.[30]

Second, Chinese scholars attribute the strained bilateral relations to Japan's "provocative" foreign policies. On the one hand, the strengthened Japan–US alliance has made Japan a key player in America's containment strategy against China.[31] On the other hand, Japan's provocative policies in the Diaoyu/Senkaku Islands as well as its possible involvement in the South China Sea also are a constant irritant to the relationship.[32] Chu Shulong argues that in the short run, Japan poses the most serious threat to China's national security and territorial integrity. More importantly, Chu argues, Japan also perceives China as its main security threat and competitor.[33]

Last but not least, Chinese scholars argue that the rise of right-wing political forces in Japan's domestic politics as well as the strong historical revisionism regarding World War II history are the two major obstacles in bilateral relations between China and Japan.[34] Huang Dahui and Jin Xiaofeng suggest that Japan's right-wing forces have steadily strengthened Japan's relationship with Taiwan. This policy behavior will seriously damage future bilateral relations between China and Japan.[35]

It is striking to note that all of the Chinese scholars whose articles we analyzed blame Japan for the deterioration of bilateral relations between the two nations. In the words of Fan Xiaoju, "from a historical perspective, Japan is always the one that causes troubles in bilateral relations." Therefore, Fan argues, Japan must make efforts to ensure the future stability of bilateral relations.[36] However, it is not a given that Japan is the only one responsible for the existing tensions. For better or worse, it takes two to tango. This seemingly one-sided view in the scholarly publications differs from the more balanced view that emerges from the surveys. This may not bode well for the future bilateral relations if policy makers in both countries take more stock of the confrontational views from the scholarly publications.

On China–India relations, Chinese scholars were optimistic until the 2017 Doklam crisis. In 2013–2016, most publications highlighted the cooperative side of the bilateral relations and downplayed potential problems. For example, Li Li argued that China–India relations had moved to a "mature stage" with three distinctive features: establishing a strategic framework for mutual cooperation; consistently building trust and solving problems; and deepening and broadening cooperation and exchanges between the two societies.[37] Similarly, Gan Junxian suggested there was a mix of "cooperation and competition" between China and India. In the short run, the two countries might have some problems, such as their respective infrastructure plans in the region. However, in the long run, China's Belt and Road Initiative (BRI) would benefit India's economic development and upgrade China–India relations to a new level.[38]

After the Doklam military standoff in 2017, however, Chinese scholars started to paint a darker picture. Hu Shisheng argues that the Doklam crisis reflects the deep-rooted strategic distrust between the two nations.[39] Wang Xiaowen suggests that Modi's great-power strategy will have some negative impacts on China–India relations. In particular, India's pursuit of regional dominance in South Asia may trigger strategic competition between China and India.[40] In a similar vein, Zhang Jiasheng argues that India is deeply suspicious of China's expanding influence in the Indian Ocean.[41] Ye Hailin even warns that no matter how China tries to improve its relationship with India, Modi's heavy-handed policy toward China will not change, and therefore strategic competition between the two nations is inevitable.[42]

The ASEAN states, as China's close neighbors, have significant status in China's foreign policy. Our textual analyses of Chinese publications indicate that Chinese scholars stress the importance of bilateral relations with ASEAN. Despite the South China Sea disputes, scholars are still optimistic about China's future relationship with ASEAN, and this is consistent with our survey findings. Most scholars highlight the importance of economic cooperation. Interestingly, some propose two new arenas where China should strengthen cooperation with ASEAN. Cai Penghong suggests that China should promote maritime cooperation with ASEAN states to enhance mutual trust between the two parties.[43] Conversely, Li Lin argues that China should enhance security and defense cooperation with ASEAN.[44]

On China's relations with the EU, Africa, and Latin America, our textual analyses have similar findings to our survey research. Overall, Chinese scholars hold optimistic views on these bilateral relations. For example, Song Hong suggests that China has deepened its strategic partnership with the EU, and that in the future, China should encourage the EU to adopt a foreign policy independent from America's.[45] According to Chinese scholars, China's BRI will be conducive to the future improvement of its bilateral relations with the EU.[46] It is worth noting that some scholars also point out potential problems between the two sides, such as strategic competition, a spillover effect from the Ukraine crisis, and the unbalanced development between the close China–Eastern Europe relations on the one side and the lukewarm China–Western Europe relations on the other.[47]

On China's relations with Africa and Latin America, most Chinese scholars highlight the positive side of economic cooperation, which is consistent with our survey research findings.[48] Still, some Chinese scholars point out potential difficulties in China's foreign relations with these two regions. For example, Tang Xiaoyang notes that China's agricultural aid and assistance to Africa have increased dramatically in recent years, but the effectiveness and sustainability of the assistance and the related aid programs still need to be improved; this is a common issue for international aid programs around the world.[49] On China–Latin America relations, Wu Hongying argues that the 2014 China–Latin America forum signifies an upgrading of their cooperation model from bilateralism to multilateralism. However, strategic cooperation between the two parties still needs to be strengthened further in the future.[50]

CONCLUSION

Relying on both our four-year survey data and textual analyses of Chinese scholarly publications, we have examined Chinese IR scholars' perceptions of and views on China's foreign policy principles and practices as well as its bilateral relations with other countries. Our survey research shows that most Chinese IR scholars are positive and satisfied about China's foreign policy practices in general and agree that China's foreign policy has become more assertive. With respect to bilateral relations, Chinese IR scholars give high scores to China's relationships with Africa, Russia, the EU, ASEAN, and Latin America but are much less optimistic with respect to India and Japan.

Most of these findings are consistent with our textual analyses of scholarly writings, but there are some notable discrepancies. In particular, while the majority of Chinese scholars in our surveys believed that China should adjust its TGYH principle and establish military alliances, in their publications we saw more diverse and nuanced arguments. There was also more faithful adherence to official government policies in the publications than in the surveys. We see this in the writings on China's North Korea policy as well as the strong tendency to blame the other parties for problems in Chinese bilateral relations, consistent with what we found in Chap. 3.

While some of the discrepancies can be explained by how the survey questionnaires were designed, the fact that most Chinese IR scholars are reluctant to publicly criticize China's foreign policy in printed publications reveals a deeper problem for both academic research and policy making. On the one hand, the self-censorship in printed publications increases the practical difficulties for scholars doing research on Chinese foreign policy using Chinese scholarly publications (and, to a lesser extent, personal interviews); we cannot reliably infer from these publications what Chinese scholars really think (and are willing to articulate in an anonymous survey), especially with regard to sensitive foreign policy issues. How to overcome this difficulty will be a new challenge for Chinese scholars in the future, especially if doing surveys like ours ceases to be a viable option.

On the other hand, the lack of critical academic evaluations and input on China's foreign policy will not only detach the government from society but also impact the effectiveness and capacity for self-reflection of China's decision-making mechanisms when it comes to foreign policy. This is not to suggest that without academic scholars, policy makers cannot develop wise and effective foreign policy. However, with public academic debates and input, China's foreign policy decision-making processes will become more effective and efficient in connecting Chinese society with the rest of the world.

NOTES

1. John Pomfret, "China's Strident Tone Raises Concerns among Western Governments," *Washington Post*, 31 January 2010; Jane Perlez, "Beijing's Exhibiting New Assertiveness in South China Sea," *New York Times*, 31 May 2012; Michael Swaine, "Perceptions of an Assertive China," *China Leadership Monitor*, No. 32 (May 2010); Kai He and Huiyun Feng, "Debating China's Assertiveness: Taking China's Power and Interests Seriously," *International Politics* 49, no. 5 (2012): 633–644; Alastair Iain Johnston, "How new and assertive is China's new assertiveness?" *International Security* 37, no. 4 (2013): 7–48; Dingding Chen, Xiaoyu Pu, and Alastair Iain Johnston. "Debating China's assertiveness." *International Security* 38, no. 3 (2014): 176–183.
2. See, for example, Elizabeth C. Economy, "The game changer: coping with China's foreign policy revolution." *Foreign Affairs* (2010): 142–152; Angela Poh and Mingjiang Li. "A China in transition: The rhetoric and substance of Chinese foreign policy under Xi Jinping." *Asian Security* 13, no. 2 (2017): 84–97. For a rebuttal, see Dingding Chen and Jianwei Wang. "Lying low no more? China's new thinking on the Tao Guang Yang Hui strategy." *China: An International Journal* 9, no. 02 (2011): 195–216.
3. Feng Zhang, "China's new thinking on alliances." *Survival* 54, no. 5 (2012): 129–148.
4. Yan Xuetong, "Cong nanhai wenti shuodao zhongguo waijiao tiaozheng" [From the South China Sea Problem to the Adjustment of China's Foreign Policy], *Shijie Zhishi* [World Affairs], no. 1, 2012, p. 33. Quoted in Feng Zhang, "China's new thinking on alliances."
5. Alec Luhn and Terry Macalister, "Russia Signs 30-Year Deal Worth $400bn to Deliver Gas to China," *The Guardian*, 21 May 2014, available at: https://www.theguardian.com/world/2014/may/21/russia-30-year-400bn-gas-deal-china.
6. For the "trawler collision" and "island nationalization" crises see Kai He, *China's Crisis Behavior* (Cambridge: Cambridge University Press, 2016).
7. Huiyun Feng and Kai He, eds. *US-China Competition and the South China Sea Disputes* (London: Routledge, 2018).
8. Nicola Smith, "India-China border brawl: Superpowers throw stones at each other as tensions heighten", *The Telegraph*. 20 August 2017. https://www.telegraph.co.uk/news/2017/08/20/india-china-border-brawl-superpowers-throw-stones-tensions-heighten/.

9. Xinhua News, 2 July 2015. http://www.gov.cn/zhengce/2015-07/02/content_2889024.htm.

10. Xinhua News, 4 December 2015. http://www.xinhuanet.com//world/2015-12/04/c_1117363082.htm.

11. Xinhua News, 28 November 2018, http://www.xinhuanet.com/world/2018-11/29/c_1123786863.htm.

12. Zhang Ruizhuang, "World Structural Change and China's Position," *Contemporary International Relations*, no. 4 (2013): 20–22. 张睿壮:《国际格局变化与中国定位》,《现代国际关系》 2013 年第 4 期, 第 20–22 页.

13. Liu Jianhua, "American Changing Asian Policy and Motives: An Analysis Based on Long-Term Cycles," *Journal of Contemporary Asia-Pacific Studies*, no. 3 (2013): 23–52. 刘建华:《美国亚太政策的交替演变及其动因探析——基于长时段周期视角的考察》,《当代亚太》 2013 年第 3 期, 第 23–52 页.

14. Liu Jiangyong, "China's Neighborhood Diplomacy: Be Creative Based on Tradition," *Contemporary International Relations*, no. 10 (2013): 28–30. 刘江永:《中国周边外交:在继承中发展创新》,《现代国际关系》 2013 年第 10 期, 第 28–30 页.

15. Yang Chuang 杨闯cited in Zheng Xuefei, "Notes from Constructing a New Type of Major Power Relations Symposium," *Contemporary International Relations*, no. 11 (2013): 61–62. 郑雪飞 :《"新型大国关系构建与国际秩序转型"研讨会综述》,《现代国际关系》 2013 年第 11 期, 第 61–62 页. ; Niu Xinchun, "Chinese Diplomacy in Need of Strategic Change," *Contemporary International Relations*, no. 1 (2013): 1–8. 牛新春,《中国外交需要战略转型》,《现代国际关系》 2013 年第 1 期, 第 1–8 页.

16. See Wu Zhicheng, "China Should Pay More Attention to Strategic Planning in its Neighboring Diplomacy," *Contemporary International Relations*, no. 1 (2015): 25–27. 吴志成:《中国周边外交需更加重视战略谋划》,《现代国际关系》 2015 年第 1 期, 第 25–27 页.

17. He Lan, "Analyzing the Current Situation and Strategic Thoughts on the China Century," *Contemporary International Relations*, no. 1 (2015): 21–23. 何兰: 《审时度势应对"中国世纪"的战略思考》, 《现代国际关系》 2015 年第 1 期, 第 21–23 页. ; Chen Xiangyang, "Some Thoughts on the World's Grand Transformation and China's Response," *Contemporary International Relations*, no. 11 (2018): 1–8. See also Ran Zongze, "What Kind of Neighborhood Does China Want to Construct," *China International Studies*, no. 2 (2014): 11–26. 阮宗泽:《中国需要构建怎样的周边》,《国际问题研究》 2014 年第 2 期, 第 11–26 页.

18. Chen Zhimin, "Does China Need a Diplomatic Revolution in Innovating its Diplomacy?" *World Economics and Politics*, no. 12 (2014): 37. 陈志敏:《中国的外交创新是否需要外交革命》,《世界经济与政治》 2014 年第 12 期, 第 37 页.

19. Liu Bowen and Fang Changping, "Neighborhood Friend Network and China's Security Environment," *Journal of Contemporary Asia-Pacific Studies*, no. 3 (2016): 68–100. 刘博文、方长平：《周边伙伴关系网络与中国周边安全环境》,《当代亚太》2016 年第 3 期, 第 68–100 页.

20. Ling Shengli, "Why Is China not Forming Alliances?" *Foreign Affairs Review*, no. 3 (2013): 29–33. 凌胜利：《中国为什么不结盟?》,《外交评论》2013 年第 3 期, 第 22–26 页、第 29–33 页.

21. Zhen Ni and Chen Zhimin, "The Non-Interference Principle and China's Voting Practice at the UNSC in the Post-Cold War Era," *China International Studies*, no. 3 (2014): 21–36. 甄妮、陈志敏：《"不干涉内政"原则与冷战后中国在安理会的投票实践》,《国际问题研究》2014 年第 3 期, 第 21–36 页.

22. Zhang Qi, "China in Reform and Humanitarian Intervention," *World Economics and Politics*, no. 4 (2015): 121. 张旗：《变革中的中国与人道主义干预》,《世界经济与政治》2015 年第 4 期, 第 121 页.

23. Huiyun Feng, Kai He, and Yan Xuetong, eds. *Chinese Scholars and Foreign Policy: Debating International Relations* (Abingdon: Routledge, 2019); Li Zhiyong, "Normative Discussions and Negotiated Intervention: China's Remodelling of the Non-Intervention Principle," *Journal of Contemporary Asia-Pacific Studies*, no. 3 (2015): 130–155. 李志永：《规范争论与协商介入: 中国对不干涉内政规范的重塑》,《当代亚太》2015 年第 3 期, 第 130–155 页.

24. Lin Limin and Zheng Yu, "North Korea's Fourth Nuclear Tests and the Changing Situation of Northeast Asia," *Contemporary International Relations*, no. 5 (2016): 1–9. 林利民、郑雨：《朝鲜第四次核试与东北亚新变局》,《现代国际关系》2016 年的 5 期, 第 1–9 页; Yang Xiyu, "The Korean Issue and China's North Korean Policy," *Contemporary International Relations*, no. 1 (2017): 15–24. 杨希雨：《朝鲜核问题与中国的对朝政策》,《现代国际关系》2017 年第 1 期, 第 15–24 页.

25. Li Meihua and Zhang Zhenting, "Major Points from the Symposium on 'Constructing Security Institutions of Peace in Northeast Asia—on North Korean Studies in 2015,'" *Contemporary International Relations*, no. 5 (2015): 61–62. 李梅花、张振亭：《东北亚和平安全机制的构建—朝鲜半岛研究 2015 高峰论坛纪要》,《现代国际关系》2015 年第 5 期, 第 61–62 页.

26. Charles Clover, "China Gives Academics Free Rein to Debate North Korea," *Financial Times*, 30 January 2018. http://www.xinhuanet.com/world/2018-11/29/c_1123786863.htm.

27. Jiao Yiqiang, "From Cognitive Discrepancy to Working Consensus: China and Russia 'One Belt One Ally' Connection Research—from an Imbalanced Perspective," *Journal of Contemporary Asia-Pacific Studies*, no. 4 (2018): 51–85. 焦一强：《由认知分歧到合作共识: 中俄"一带一盟"对接合作研

究—基于不对称性相互依赖的视角》,《当代亚太》 2018 年第 4 期, 第 51–85 页.

28. Shi Ze, "Building Strong China-Russian Energy Strategic Partnership," *China International Studies*, no. 5 (2015): 26–37. 石泽: 《构建牢固的中俄能源战略伙伴关系》,《国际问题研究》 2015 年第 5 期, 第 26–37 页.

29. Wang Shuchun and Liu Sisi, "Russia's New Asian Strategy and its Impact on China-Russian Relations," *Journal of Contemporary Asia-Pacific Studies*, no. 6 (2015): 82–100. 王树春、刘思思: 《俄罗斯新亚洲战略及其对中俄关系的影响》,《当代亚太》 2015 年第 6 期, 第 82–100 页.

30. Li Xiangyang, "Trends of China's Neighbouring Development," *Contemporary International Relations*, no. 1 (2015): 12–14. 李向阳: 《中国周边环境的发展趋势》,《现代国际关系》 2015 年第 1 期, 第 12–14 页.

31. Men Honghua, "Japan's Changing Situation and Future China–Japan Relations," *World Economics and Politics*, no. 1 (2016): 72. 门洪华: 《日本变局与中日关系的走向》,《世界经济与政治》 2016 年第 1 期, 第 72 页; Miao Ji and Li Fujian, "Strategic Rejection and Strategic Adjustment: Japanese and Australian Responses towards China's Rise," *Foreign Affairs Review*, no. 1 (2014): 72–82. 苗吉、李福建: 《战略拒戒与战略调适: 日澳对中国崛起的反应》,《外交评论》 2014 年第 1 期, 第 72–82 页.

32. Zhu Haiyan, "Japan's Interference into the South China Sea: Trends and Implications," *China International Studies*, no. 2 (2016): 126. 朱海燕: 《日本介入南海问题的动向及影响》,《国际问题研究》 2016 年第 2 期, 第 126 页.

33. Chu Shulong, "Japan's National Security Strategy and China's Japan Strategy," *Contemporary International Relations*, no. 1 (2014): 11–13. 楚树龙: 《日本国家战略及中国对日战略》,《现代国际关系》 2014 年第 1 期, 第 11–13 页.

34. Tang Yanlin and Zhang Lei, "Japanese Politics and the Future of China–Japan Relations," *Contemporary International Relations*, no. 3 (2015): 39–45. 唐彦林、张磊: 《日本政局与中日关系走向》,《现代国际关系》 2015 年第 3 期, 第 39–45 页.

35. Huang Dahui and Jin Xiaofeng, "Leaning More to the Right and the Evolution of Japan's Pro-Taiwan Political Forces," *Foreign Affairs Review*, no. 3 (2017): 50–76. 黄大慧、金肖丰: 《政治右倾化与冷战后日本政界亲台势力的演变》,《外交评论》 2017 年第 3 期, 第 50–76 页.

36. Fan Xiaoju, "Responding to Old and New Problems in China–Japan Relations: Thoughts on Achieving Completely Normal China-Japan Relations," *Contemporary International Relations*, no. 10 (2018): 1–7. 樊小菊: 《应对中日关系的新形势与老问题—实现中日关系"完全正常化"的思考》,《现代国际关系》 2018 年第 10 期, 第 1–7 页.

37. Li Li, "Exploring the Reasons for the China–India Relationship Moving Towards a Mature Bilateral Relationship," *Contemporary International Relations*, no. 3 (2013): 49–55. 李莉: 《中印关系走向成熟及其原因探析》, 《现代国际关系》 2013 年第 3 期, 第 49–55 页.

38. Gan Junxian, "One Belt One Road: Will the Dragon and Elephant Dance Together? *China International Studies*, no. 4 (2015): 96–113. 甘均先: 《"一带一路": 龙象独行抑或共舞?》, 《国际问题研究》 2015 年第 4 期, 第 96–113 页.

39. Hu Shisheng, "Doklam Standoff Crisis and Future China-India Relations," *Contemporary International Relations*, no. 11 (2017): 9–22. 胡仕胜: 《洞朗对峙危机与中印关系的未来》, 《现代国际关系》 2017 年第 11 期, 第 9–22 页.

40. Wang Xiaowen, "Analysing Modi's Great Power Strategy," *Contemporary International Relations*, no. 5 (2017): 33–42. 王晓文: 《印度莫迪政府的大国战略评析》, 《现代国际关系》 2017 年第 5 期, 第 33–42 页.

41. Li Jiasheng, "Meeting in the Indian Ocean: The Logic of the Indian Response to China Entering the Indian Ocean," *World Economics and Politics*, no. 9 (2017): 37–61. 李家胜: 《印度洋相遇—印度应对中国进入印度洋的行为逻辑》, 《世界经济与政治》 2017 年第 9 期, 第 37–61 页.

42. Ye Hailin, "China's Rise and Response to Challenges from a Secondary Strategic Focus: The China-India Relationship after Doklam," *World Economics and Politics*, no. 4 (2018): 122. 叶海林: 《中国崛起与次要战略方向挑战的应对—以洞朗事件后的中印关系为例》, 《世界经济与政治》 2018 年第 4 期, 第 122 页.

43. Cai Penghong, "China-ASEAN Maritime Cooperation: Process, Motivations and Future," *China International Studies*, no. 4 (2015): 14–25. 蔡鹏鸿: 《中国—东盟海洋合作 : 进程、动因和前景》, 《国际问题研究》 2015 年第 4 期, 第 14–25 页.

44. Liu Lin, "Looking into China and ASEAN Defense Cooperation," *China International Studies*, no. 3 (2017): 16–26. 刘琳: 《中国与东盟国家防务合作探析》, 《国际问题研究》 2017 年第 3 期, 第 16–26 页.

45. Song Hong, "Great Power Cooperation and Competition in an International System of One Superpower and Many Major Powers," *Journal of Contemporary Asia-Pacific Studies*, no. 4 (2016): 4–24. 宋泓: 《一超多强国际格局下的大国合作与纷争》, 《当代亚太》 2016 年第 4 期, 第 4–24 页.

46. Feng Zhongping and Huang Jing, "The motivations, current situation and future of China and Europe cooperation on the Belt and Road Initiative," in *Contemporary International Relations*, no. 2 (2016): 9–15. 冯仲平、黄静: 《中欧"一带一路"合作的动力、现状与前景》, 《现代国际关系》 2016 年第 2 期, 第 9–15 页.

47. Xu Gang, "China and Central and Eastern European Relations: New Stage, New Challenge and a New Way of Thinking," *Contemporary International Relations*, no. 2 (2015): 39–45. 徐刚: 《中国与中东欧国家关系: 新阶段、新挑战与新思路》, 《现代国际关系》 2015 年第 2 期, 第 39–45 页.

48. Liu Hongwu, "The future of African Development and China's Strategic choice," in *China International Studies*, no. 2 (2013): 72–87. 刘鸿武: 《非洲发展大势与中国的战略选择》, 《国际问题研究》 2013 年第 2 期, 第 72–87 页. Luo Jianbo, "China-African Relations and China's Global Responsibility," in *World Politics and Economics*, no. 9 (2013): 52. 罗建波: 《中非关系与中国的世界责任》, 《世界政治与经济》 2013 年第 9 期, 第 52 页. Chai Yu, "The Internationalization of the RMB based on empirical research in Latin America" in *World Politics and Economics*, no. 4 (2013): 78. 柴瑜: 《人民币国际化与拉美作为对象区域的考察》, 《世界政治与经济》 2013 年第 4 期, 第 78 页. Jiang Shixue, "Thoughts on Ways to Build China-Latin American Community of Common Destiny," in *China International Studies*, no. 2 (2018): 30–42. 江时学: 《构建中国与拉美命运共同体路径思考》, 《国际问题研究》 2018 年第 2 期, 第 30–42 页. Huang Yupei, "Building China-African Economic and Trade Cooperation Zones: Challenges and Ways Forward," in *China International Studies*, no. 4 (2018): 112–126. 黄玉沛: 《中非经贸合作区建设: 挑战与深化路径》, 《国际问题研究》 2018 年第 4 期, 第 112–126 页.

49. Tang Xiaoyang, "Evolution and Impact of China's Agricultural Aid Forms to Africa," *World Economics and Politics*, no. 5 (2013): 56–69. 唐晓阳: 《中国对非洲农业援助形式的演变及其效果》, 《世界政治与经济》 2013 年第 5 期, 第 56–69 页.

50. Wu Hongying, "Upgrading of China-Latin American Relations," *Contemporary International Relations*, no. 2 (2015): 19–21. 吴洪英: 《中拉关系正在"升级换代"》, 《现代国际关系》 2015 年第 2 期, 第 19–21 页.

CHAPTER 5

Understanding China's Rise Through the Eyes of Scholars and Beyond

For centuries, China has been a myth for the outside world. It is one of the oldest civilizations in the world, yet the People's Republic is also young, with only 70 years of history. Its political system is opaque to outsiders and even to people within the country, yet it has experienced spectacular economic growth in the past four decades. Napoleon once warned, "China is a sleeping lion. Let her sleep, for when she wakes, she will shake the world." Will China's rise lead to a shake-up of the existing world order, resulting in more conflicts as it runs head to head with the reigning hegemon? Or is China, as it often claims, a blessing to the world and well on the road to becoming a responsible great power? The answers to these questions are not straightforward, because scholars and policy makers continue to ponder and debate what China wants now as well as what China will want in the future.[1] If anything, China offers a mixed set of images to the outside world.

Since the 2008 global financial crisis, especially after Chinese President Xi Jinping came to power in 2013, Chinese engagement with the world has taken an assertive turn from the Deng Xiaoping era's "*Taoguang Yanghui*" (keeping a low profile)—the long-time guiding principle in Chinese foreign policy—to "*you suo zuo wei*" (striving for achievement).[2] In handling maritime and territorial disputes with neighboring states, China has displayed heavy-handed approaches, especially in the Diaoyu/Senkaku Islands dispute with Japan and the Scarborough Shoal dispute

© The Author(s) 2019
H. Feng et al., *How China Sees the World*,
https://doi.org/10.1007/978-981-15-0482-2_5

with the Philippines. In 2015, China launched a five-year reform program to modernize the People's Liberation Army, which includes improving its capacity, conducting joint operations, and protecting Chinese business interests and citizens abroad. China has also become more vocal in the United Nations Security Council (UNSC), exercising its veto power more frequently over issues regarding Iran, North Korea, and Syria.

In the economic arena, however, China has initiated a diplomatic wave of "charm offensives" by increasing its investment and economic activities in the African continent and Latin America. In 2013, China launched the Belt and Road Initiative (BRI), its massive global development strategy, focusing on infrastructure development and investments across Asia, Europe, Africa, the Middle East, and the Americas. In March 2015, China established the Asian Infrastructure Investment Bank (AIIB) with 57 countries as founding members, including developed economies such as the United Kingdom, Germany, France, Italy, Australia, and South Korea, to support sustainable infrastructure and other productive sectors in Asia and beyond.[3] In 2017, President Xi was applauded at the Davos World Economic Forum for signaling China's willingness to remain a strong defender of free trade and globalization, contrary to Trump's "America First" policy and US economic protectionism.[4]

With these seemingly contradictory behaviors, what does China really want? In the previous three chapters, we sought to shed new light on this question by integrating opinion surveys of Chinese international relations (IR) scholars at several consecutive Chinese Community of Political Science and International Studies (CCPSIS) annual conferences (2014–2017) with textual analyses of their published work (2013–2018). The results offer new perspectives for understanding China's perceptions of and views on international relations, through the eyes of Chinese IR scholars and, by extension, Chinese policy makers. Here, we highlight three main findings. First, Chinese IR scholars hold a pragmatic and somewhat conflicted view about China's own power in the international system. They are confident that national rejuvenation is China's destiny, and they see their country as moving toward that goal. They are also fully aware that structural competition between the current hegemon and the rising state—that is, the United States and China—is inevitable as China narrows the power gap between the two nations. Nevertheless, they do not think that China will replace America's hegemony anytime soon, though they believe that the United States' decline is inevitable.

Second, there is a broad consensus among Chinese IR scholars that the biggest challenges in Chinese foreign policy remain unsettled sovereignty issues in terms of national reunification, border demarcation, and disputed territorial and maritime claims with neighboring states in the Asia-Pacific region. They also see the potential of the United States getting involved in some of these conflicts, especially in the Taiwan Strait, the East China Sea, and the South China Sea. However, Chinese IR scholars in general do not think conflict is the dominant theme between the two nations; rather, they are cautiously optimistic that issues of common interest can serve as a foundation of cooperation between China and the United States. Thus, most Chinese IR scholars hold a relatively neutral view about both present and future US–China relations.

Third, Chinese IR scholars are confident about China's foreign policy practices as well as its bilateral relations with other major countries and regions. However, they seem to be divided over whether China should adopt a more proactive foreign policy stance by changing its "keeping-a-low-profile" principle and taking up more responsibilities, or should, in the Chinese phrase, "strive for achievement"; the latter would be a major departure from China's traditional diplomatic practices, which included declining to form alliances and to interfere in other nations' internal affairs. A hotly debated question among scholars is whether China and Russia, in the face of common US pressures, should form a formal alliance. These contested views among Chinese IR scholars on the principles and practices of China's foreign policy might well reflect the lack of consensus among Chinese policy makers on how to grapple with their nation's increased power and status in the international arena, as well as its dynamic relations with other states, especially the United States.

In the remainder of this concluding chapter, we first examine how Chinese IR scholars perceive the international environment, using three questions from the survey. Specifically, we asked respondents: (1) whether they see the international environment as more friendly or hostile than in the past; (2) which countries they think pose the greatest threats to China's national security; and (3) which country is the most likely to enter into a conflict or even a war with China in coming years. After analyzing scholars' perceptions of the international environment, we then discuss the implications of these findings for the future of US–China relations. We conclude that despite the escalating trade war between the two nations, the United States and China are not doomed to fall into Thucydides's Trap.

CHINA IN THE WORLD: FRIENDS AND THREATS

In both official statements and the popular media, "old friend of the Chinese people" is a phrase affectionately bestowed on individuals (leaders or people having special relationships with China) deemed to have formed a long-term friendship with the People's Republic through either hard times, such as fighting wars, or sharing similar values and positions. Fostering friendships with both developing and developed countries has been a major objective of China's foreign policy. After all, having more friends suggests a more benign external environment, which is conducive to China's economic development. The official line of the Chinese government is that with its massive infrastructural investments across the world, especially the BRI, China is building a community of shared destiny, and its circle of friends is expanding. For example, China's official media have claimed that "China and Latin America and the Caribbean States (LAC) are becoming close friends through BRI."[5]

Are Chinese IR scholars in agreement with such rhetoric? In our surveys, we asked participants: "Does China have true friends in the world?" Across the four years of our survey, only about a third of surveyed participants (34%) believed that China has true friends, while exactly half of them did not (Fig. 5.1).[6] These views were quite consistent over time, with a

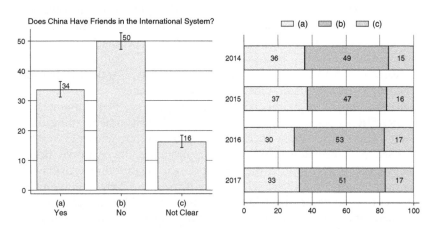

Fig. 5.1 China's international friendships. Note: The left panel plots the distribution of the responses with 95% confidence intervals over the four-year period. The right panel plots the responses in each individual year of the survey. The numbers are in percentage points and may not add up to 100 due to rounding

slight dip in 2016 in the percentage of participants who believed that China has true friends. As mentioned in the previous chapters, this may be attributable to the diplomatic setbacks China experienced that year, especially the Hague ruling and China's relative diplomatic isolation in the aftermath. These results indicate that in the eyes of Chinese IR scholars, China's external environment is not as friendly as the Chinese government claims. Their pessimism seems to resonate with the Pew Global Survey in 2018, where 43% of participants surveyed in 25 countries expressed unfavorable views toward China.[7]

We also gave participants the opportunity to specify which countries they deemed China's true friends. Consistently over the four years of our surveys, participants singled out Pakistan as the "iron friend" (巴铁 *Ba Tie*) of China. Other countries mentioned occasionally were Israel, Cambodia, and Russia. It is interesting that not a single respondent listed North Korea as a true friend of China, contrary to China's official line. Similar to our findings on China's North Korea policy in the previous chapter, it is clear that Chinese IR scholars now regard North Korea as more of a liability than a friend.

We further asked participants to assess China's security threats more directly by selecting which country they thought will pose the greatest threat to China's national security and which is the most likely to run into military conflict or even war with China in the next five years. For both questions, we gave respondents a list of countries but also gave them the option of naming one not included in the list, though almost no one took that option. While the wording of the questions implied that they should pick one country only, some respondents chose more than one country, especially for the question on the threat to China's national security.

Figure 5.2 shows the results for the question on threats that other countries pose to China's national security over time. The rankings of threat perceptions based on the proportion of positive responses were stable through the first three years of the survey. In 2014, the three countries perceived as most threatening to China's national security were: the United States (47%), Japan (39%), and North Korea (16%). Surprisingly, 12% of the respondents named Russia as the greatest threat. None of the remaining countries in the list (Australia, India, the Philippines, the United Kingdom, and Vietnam) was chosen by more than 5%. In 2015, the country ranking stayed the same with some small changes in the percentages, none of which is statistically significant. In 2016, the proportion of respondents perceiving the United States as the greatest threat increased

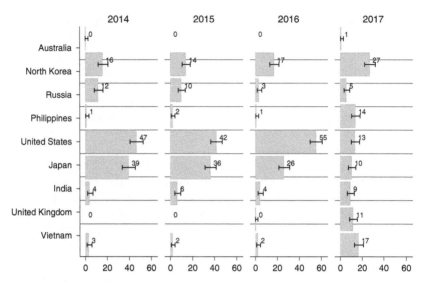

Fig. 5.2 Biggest threats to China's national security. Note: The horizontal bars with 95% confidence intervals are percentages of respondents saying that the particular country is the biggest threat to China's national security. The percentages add up to over 100 as some respondents chose multiple countries

(from 42% in 2015 to 55%), while that of Japan decreased (from 36% to 26%), but the rankings of the top three remain unchanged.

The responses in 2017 contrast dramatically with the patterns in the first three years. Rather than concentrating on a few countries, the votes were more evenly distributed. Six of the nine countries were selected by more than 10% of the respondents as posing the greatest threat to China's national security. Consequently, there was a substantial reshuffling of the rankings. North Korea (27%) became the country posing the greatest threat to China's national security, followed by two South East Asian countries—Vietnam (17%) and the Philippines (14%). The United States (13%) and Japan (10%) dropped to numbers four and six, respectively, while the United Kingdom (11%) and India (9%) both saw significant increases in their respective shares of the vote. These results suggest that Chinese IR scholars have come to view the international environment as much more complicated and uncertain, so potential threats to China's national security are perceived as coming from multiple regions over issues ranging from the South China Sea disputes to Brexit.

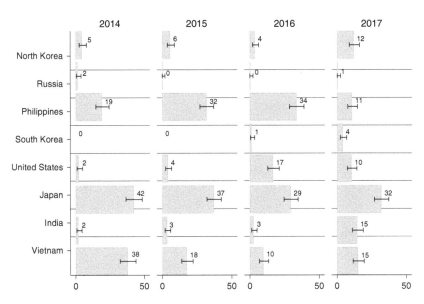

Fig. 5.3 Likelihood of conflict or war with China. Note: The horizontal bars with 95% confidence intervals are percentages of respondents saying that the particular country is the most likely to enter into a conflict or even a war with China. The percentages add up to over 100 in 2014 as some respondents chose multiple countries

A country posing threats to China's national security, however, does not necessarily mean that conflict with that country is imminent, as can be seen in Fig. 5.3, which shows the responses to the question asking Chinese IR scholars to identity the country most likely to run into military conflicts with China in the next five years. Here, a pattern similar to Fig. 5.2 emerges. Between 2014 and 2016, the responses concentrated on three countries—Japan, the Philippines, and Vietnam—that traded places in the top three list. In 2017, however, the responses were more evenly distributed. Six out of the eight countries received more than 10% of the vote, with India cracking the top three, followed closely by North Korea, the Philippines, and the United States.

When we combine the results from Figs. 5.2 and 5.3, an interesting observation is that the United States—the country Chinese IR scholars perceived as posing the greatest threat to China's national security overall—was ranked much lower in terms of the likelihood of direct military confrontation with China in the near future, though it is possible that the United States could be indirectly dragged into future military conflicts in the East and South China Seas. Still, if the perceptions of Chinese IR scholars can indeed reflect some of what Chinese leaders think, we do not see China drawing up concrete plans to fight with the United States, as Michael Pillsbury has suggested.[8]

RETHINKING THE US–CHINA RIVALRY[9]

Going back to one of the main questions raised in Chap. 1, the evidence we have presented so far in this book—the views and perceptions of Chinese IR scholars on China's power, China's foreign policy, and China–US relations in both the opinion surveys and their published work—seems to suggest that at least from the Chinese perspective, it is possible for China and the United States to escape the so-called Thucydides' Trap—inevitable military conflicts between the existing hegemon and a rising power.[10] The one caveat to this conclusion is that our survey ended in July 2017. And the world has certainly changed much since then.

Most notably, we have witnessed the potential danger of conflicts between the United States and China since early 2018. The escalating trade war as well as the emerging "technology war" around Huawei and 5G have led to increasing concerns about a "new kind of Cold War" emanating from the US–China rivalry.[11] The 2017 US National Security Strategy labeled China a revisionist state, because it "challenge[s] American power, influence, and interests, attempting to erode American security and prosperity."[12] As we have mentioned in our previous chapters, some Chinese scholars also suggest that US–China competition is a "structural contradiction," originating from the transformation of the international order due to China's rise and America's decline.[13] Are the two countries destined for a path of destruction?

Certainly, nuclear weapons and mutually assured destruction have rendered a large-scale war too costly for both the United States and China, although we cannot rule out the possibility of military clashes between the two in some regional hot spots, such as the Taiwan Strait and even the South China Sea. These are indeed the issue areas that deeply concern Chinese IR scholars when considering a possible armed conflict between the United States and China. Setting aside third-party factors drawing the major powers into a conflict, however, what are the United States and China really competing for in world politics?

The ongoing trade war suggests the competition is occurring in the economic realm. When Trump launched the trade war against China, the rationale was to strengthen the US economy and "Make America Great Again." But the results of the conflict over trade are still not clear, because globalization and deepening economic interdependence have blurred the line between losses and gains in international trade. For example, many Chinese exports to the United States are actually manufactured by US companies operating in China. Although Trump's high tariffs on Chinese exports will certainly hurt the Chinese economy, they will also have a negative impact on those US companies as well as America's economy in general. It is not a cliché to say that there will be no real winner in the trade war, because in economic terms, both countries will lose as a result of competing tariffs. The key question is: Who will lose more? Trump bets that China will suffer more and therefore will blink first. He might be right that China will lose more, but whether it will blink is a different and complicated issue that will be determined by many non-economic factors, such as leadership style, domestic politics, and Chinese nationalism.

Whatever the outcome of the trade war, one thing is undeniable: the United States remains the more powerful country, economically and militarily. Our research in this book also confirms that Chinese IR scholars consistently agree the United States will remain the most powerful state in the world for a relatively long time, although they believe it will decline eventually. Although China may not officially compromise with the United States, it has already further liberalized its economy and reduced regulations on foreign investments, in accordance with US demands. More importantly, China has toned down the hype about its economic growth as well as its ambitious "Made in China 2025" policy—the state-backed industrial strategy that has triggered alarm in the West. To a certain extent, for Chinese leaders, Trump's trade war has been a hard revelation of the huge power gap between China and the United States.

Beijing seems to have no other choice but to continue deepening its economic openness and market-oriented reforms, and further integrating itself into the world economy to offset the negative impacts of the trade war. If that is the case, the economic competition between the United States and China could actually help both countries reposition their status in the international system, enabling them to avoid potential miscalculations and misperceptions that might lead to unnecessary military conflicts or even war.

While it is the hope that the trade war will eventually be resolved, that will not be the end of US–China competition in the international system. Also on the line in the power play between the two giants are leadership and prestige.[14] From Trump's high-profile meetings with Kim Jong-un and Vladimir Putin, despite domestic criticism, it is clear that the US president is pursuing leadership and prestige in world politics. Trump believed that he and the associated prestige of the United States could persuade Kim to give up nuclear weapons and convince Putin to change course in Syria and Ukraine. Unfortunately, so far, America's unparalleled material power has not brought about the equivalent level of prestige to the United States in achieving what Trump wants from North Korea and Russia. A similar dilemma arose when Trump unilaterally withdrew from the Iran nuclear deal despite strong opposition from America's European allies.

Trump's failed efforts attest that international prestige should be based on persuasion and soft power. Leadership is an element of soft power and a foundation of prestige for states. Nye argues that a state's foreign policy can be a source of soft power.[15] However, this does not mean that all components of foreign policy can turn into soft power. In an anarchical international system, states are self-regarding, unitary actors. The only difference between states is material power—that is, there are superpowers, great powers, middle powers, and small powers. To win the respect and admiration of others, a state needs to do what others are unable or unwilling, but aspire and desire, to do: to solve common problems by fostering international cooperation.

But unlike military and economic power, leadership and prestige can be shared. Washington and Beijing could work together to promote shared leadership in order to achieve greater cooperation among all nations. The common problems in world politics include not only traditional challenges, such as war and interstate disputes, but also non-traditional issues, such as poverty, climate change, and pandemics. Many of these problems present opportunities for joint leadership between China and the United States. The Iran nuclear issue is one example of a "common problem" for the international community, which led to multilateral efforts and cooperation among major powers through the "P5 plus 1" mechanism (involving the five permanent members of the United

Nations Security Council, plus Germany). However, cooperation is by no means easy for self-regarding states, as we can see from Trump's decision to renege on the Iran agreement.

To regain its leadership, prestige, and credibility in the world due to Trump's erratic foreign policies, the United States needs to work with China. North Korea's nuclear crisis is a good example and was flagged by the majority of the scholars in our surveys as the top issue of mutual interest. After the failed summit meeting in Hanoi, though Trump might still keep his "very special friendship" with Kim Jong-un, there is no sign that Pyongyang is willing to give up its nuclear weapons program. Even though the United States could finally leverage its power to force Kim to give up his nuclear weapons program (which is still unlikely to happen anytime soon), helping North Korea integrate into the international community will be a tough challenge, economically and strategically, for the United States to handle alone. Other concerned states, especially China, South Korea, Japan, and Russia, need to coordinate in facilitating the peaceful settlement of the nuclear crisis on the Korean Peninsula. Therefore, the United States should consider welcoming a rising China to share some of the burdens and responsibilities of global governance that it has had to bear alone in the past.

Our research on Chinese IR scholars in this book suggests China had a benign and somewhat (overly) optimistic perception of US–China relations before the trade war. As a rising power, China indeed has a desire for a higher status and more prestige in world politics. However, this cannot be achieved with military might, as we can see from mounting criticisms of China's assertiveness in diplomacy, especially in the South China Sea. Therefore, China should also work with the United States and help identify the areas where China can play a value-added role in facilitating state cooperation, thereby enabling it to accumulate the prestige and status it deserves.

With great power comes great responsibility. This is true for China as well as for the United States. If Washington and Beijing can share international leadership, they will not only avoid "Thucydides's Trap" but also provide public goods to the whole world. Although these two countries might not have equal material power, they can have the same level of prestige in the future. A balance of prestige will play the same, if not a more important, role as a balance of power in ensuring stability and prosperity in future world politics.

Notes

1. Ross Terrill, "What Does China Want?" *Wilson Quarterly* 29, no. 4 (2005): 50–61; Jeffrey W. Legro, "What China Will Want: The Future Intentions of a Rising Power," *Perspectives on Politics* 5, no. 3 (2007): 515–534; Timothy R. Heath, "What Does China Want? Discerning the PRC's National Strategy," *Asian Security* 8, no. 1 (2012): 54–72.

2. Yan Xuetong, "From Keeping a Low Profile to Striving for Achievement," *The Chinese Journal of International Politics* 7, no. 2 (2014): 153–184.

3. Kai He and Huiyun Feng, "Leadership Transition and Global Governance: Role Conception, Institutional Balancing, and the AIIB," *The Chinese Journal of International Politics* 12, no. 2 (2019): 153–178.

4. "Xi Jinping signals China will champion free trade if Trump builds barriers," The *Guardian*, 18 January 2017. https://www.theguardian.com/business/2017/jan/17/china-xi-jinping-china-free-trade-trump-globalisation-wef-davos.

5. Pan Deng, "China and LAC are becoming close friends through BRI," *China Global Television Network* (CGTN), 28 April 2019. https://news.cgtn.com/news/3d3d514f32457a4d34457a6333566d54/index.html.

6. The term "true friend" might have contributed to the low sense of friendship. In Chinese understanding, a "true friend" (真正的朋友) means someone you can rely on in times of difficulties and someone who will support you under any circumstance. A "true friend" also evokes a sense of loyalty and trust based on the past and history. Therefore, our question might have set too high a bar for countries to be qualified as a "true friend" of China.

7. Kat Devin, "5 Charts on Global Views of China," Pew Research Center, 19 October 2018, available at: https://www.pewresearch.org/fact-tank/2018/10/19/5-charts-on-global-views-of-china/.

8. Michael Pillsbury, *The Hundred-Year Marathon: China's Secret Strategy to Replace America as the Global Superpower* (New York: Henry Holt and Company, 2015). For a good critical review, see Alastair Iain Johnston, "Shaky Foundations: The 'Intellectual Architecture' of Trump's China Policy," *Survival* 61, no. 2 (2019): 189–202.

9. This section is based on Kai He and Huiyun Feng, "A Quest for Joint Prestige: Rethinking US–China Rivalry," *Global Asia* 13, no. 3 (2018): 80–85.

10. Graham Allison, *Destined for War: Can America and China Escape Thucydides's Trap?* (New York: Houghton Mifflin Harcourt, 2017).

11. The Economist, "A New Kind of Cold War," 16 May 2019, available at: https://www.economist.com/leaders/2019/05/16/a-new-kind-of-cold-war.

12. See The White House, "National Security Strategy of the United States of America," Washington DC, December 2017, p. 2.
13. Xuetong Yan, "From Keeping a Low Profile to Striving for Achievement," *The Chinese Journal of International Politics* 7, no. 2 (2014): 153–184.
14. Prestige is closely related to, but differs from, power. Power is about getting what you want despite resistance, but prestige is about getting others to do, and even want, what you want.
15. Joseph Nye Jr., *The Powers to Lead* (Oxford: Oxford University Press, 2008), 19.

APPENDIX: SURVEY QUESTIONNAIRE

1. 您的性别
   - (a) 男
   - (b) 女
2. 您的年龄
   - (a) 20 以下
   - (b) 21–30
   - (c) 31–40
   - (d) 41–50
   - (e) 51–60
   - (f) 60 以上
3. 您现在的职业
   - (a) 在读学生
   - (b) 高校教学/研究人员
   - (c) 专职研究人员(非高校)
   - (d) 新闻工作者/记者
   - (e) 政府官员
   - (f) 自由职业国际关系爱好者
   - (g) 其他
4. 您有国外的学习/研究经历吗 (包括短期访问学者3个月或3个月以上)?
   - (a) 有
   - (b) 没有

1. What is your gender?
   - (a) Male
   - (b) Female
2. What is your age?
   - (a) 20 or younger
   - (b) 21–30
   - (c) 31–40
   - (d) 41–50
   - (e) 51–60
   - (f) Older than 60
3. What is your current occupation?
   - (a) Full-time student
   - (b) University teaching/research staff
   - (c) Full-time researchers (non-universities)
   - (d) Journalists/reporters
   - (e) Government officials
   - (f) Freelance international relations enthusiasts
   - (g) Other
4. Do you have study/research experience abroad (including short-term visiting scholarships of three months or longer)?
   - (a) Yes
   - (b) No

(*continued*)

© The Author(s) 2019
H. Feng et al., *How China Sees the World*,
https://doi.org/10.1007/978-981-15-0482-2

(continued)

5. 您目前获得的最高学位是什么? 　(a) 本科 　(b) 研究生 　(c) 博士	5. What is your highest degree? 　(a) Undergraduate degree 　(b) Graduate degree (master's degree or equivalent) 　(c) Doctorate
6. 您是否在去年也参加了共同体 　会议? 　(a) 是 　(b) 否	6. Did you attend the CCPSIS meeting last year? 　(a) Yes 　(b) No
7. 请问您是否是中国公民? 　(a) 是 　(b) 不是	7. Are you a Chinese citizen? 　(a) Yes 　(b) No
8. 您如何评价目前美国在世界政 　治中的实力状况? 　(a) 是无可争议的世界霸主, 目 　前没有衰退迹象 　(b) 是世界霸主, 但会衰退 　(c) 已经从世界霸主的地位衰退, 　但过程会很慢 　(d) 一个很快衰退的世界霸主 　(e) 北美的地区霸主	8. How would you evaluate the power of the United 　States in the current international system? 　(a) Undisputed global hegemon with no signs of 　decline 　(b) Global hegemon but will decline 　(c) Slowly declined global hegemon in a slow 　process 　(d) Fast declined global hegemon 　(e) American regional hegemon
9. 您如何评价目前中国在世界政 　治中的实力状况? 　(a) 超级大国 　(b) 一个崛起的超级大国 　(c) 亚洲的地区霸主 　(d) 崛起中的亚洲霸主 　(e) 停滞的大国, 将会很快衰落 　(f) 不清楚	9. How would you evaluate China's power in the 　current international system? 　(a) Superpower 　(b) Rising superpower 　(c) Asian regional hegemon 　(d) Rising Asian regional hegemon 　(e) Stagnant power declining soon 　(f) Not clear
10. 您认为中国是不是在国际上有 　真正的"朋友"? 　(a) 有朋友(请注明) 　(b) 没朋友 　(c) 不清楚	10. Do you think China has true "friends" in the 　world? 　(a) Yes (please specify) 　(b) No 　(c) Not clear
11. 您认为中国在未来十年经济实 　力方面会超过美国吗? 　(a) 非常有可能 　(b) 有可能 　(c) 不太可能 　(d) 非常不可能 　(e) 不清楚	11. Do you think China will surpass the United 　States in terms of economic power in the next 　decade? 　(a) Very likely 　(b) Likely 　(c) Unlikely 　(d) Very unlikely 　(e) Not clear

(*continued*)

(continued)

12. 您认为中国未来十年军事实力方面会超过美国吗?

(a) 非常有可能
(b) 有可能
(c) 不太可能
(d) 非常不可能
(e) 不清楚

12. Do you think China will surpass the United States in terms of military power in the next decade?

(a) Very likely
(b) Likely
(c) Unlikely
(d) Very unlikely
(e) Not clear

13. 有人认为政治制度也是国家的一种实力. 您认为中国在未来十年在制度实力方面会超过美国吗?

(a) 非常有可能
(b) 有可能
(c) 不太可能
(d) 非常不可能
(e) 不清楚

13. Some people think that a political system is also a source of the power. Do you think China will surpass the United States in this power in the next decade?

(a) Very likely
(b) Likely
(c) Unlikely
(d) Very unlikely
(e) Not clear

14. 有人认为国家的文化也是一种实力. 您认为中国在未来十年在文化实力方面会超过美国吗?

(a) 非常有可能
(b) 有可能
(c) 不太可能
(d) 非常不可能
(e) 不清楚

14. Some believe that culture is also a source of power. Do you think China will surpass the United States in terms of cultural power in the next decade?

(a) Very likely
(b) Likely
(c) Unlikely
(d) Very unlikely
(e) Not clear

15. 您是否认为中国会在未来十年超过美国, 成为世界第一强国(包括经济及军事等综合实力)?

(a) 非常有可能
(b) 有可能
(c) 不太可能
(d) 非常不可能
(e) 不清楚

15. Do you think that China will surpass the United States in the next decade and become the most powerful country (in terms of comprehensive power)?

(a) Very likely
(b) Likely
(c) Unlikely
(d) Very unlikely
(e) Not clear

16. 您如何评价中美关系的现状?

(a) 非常好
(b) 一般好
(c) 不好不坏(非敌非友)
(d) 敌对关系
(e) 不清楚

16. How would you describe China–US relations now?

(a) Very good
(b) Good
(c) Neither good nor bad
(d) Antagonistic
(e) Not clear

(continued)

(continued)

17. 您如何看未来十年的中美关系?
    (a) 非常好
    (b) 一般好
    (c) 不好不坏 (非敌非友)
    (d) 敌对关系
    (e) 不清楚

17. What would Sino–US relations be in ten years?
    (a) Very good
    (b) Good
    (c) Neither good nor bad
    (d) Antagonistic
    (e) Not clear

18. 您如何评价当前的国际体系结构?
    (a) 单极世界 (其他大国短期内无法追赶或超越)
    (b) 一超多强 (其他大国有希望短期内追赶或超越)
    (c) 两极世界
    (d) 多极世界
    (e) 无极世界(没有超级大国)
    (f) 其他

18. How would you evaluate the current structure of the international system?
    (a) Unipolar (other major powers cannot catch up or surpass the superpower in the short term)
    (b) One superpower and many great powers (with hopes to catch up or surpass the superpower in the short term)
    (c) Bipolar
    (d) Multipolar
    (e) Non-polar (no superpower)
    (f) Other

19. 您认为中国在未来五年内最有可能和下述那个国家发生武装冲突甚至战争?
    (a) 朝鲜
    (b) 俄罗斯
    (c) 菲律宾
    (d) 韩国
    (e) 美国
    (f) 日本
    (g) 印度
    (h) 越南
    (i) 其他 (请注明)

19. Do you think that China is most likely to have an armed conflict or even a war with the following countries in the next five years?
    (a) North Korea
    (b) Russia
    (c) Philippines
    (d) South Korea
    (e) United States
    (f) Japan
    (g) India
    (h) Vietnam
    (i) Other (please specify)

20. 您认为下述问题中哪个/些问题是影响中美关系中最大难题?(您可以有多个选择)
    (a) 贸易争端
    (b) 货币问题
    (c) 台湾问题
    (d)人权问题
    (e) 网络安全
    (f) 民主政治问题
    (g) 能源和环境问题
    (h) 钓鱼岛争端
    (i) 南中国海问题
    (j) 其他问题(请列举)--------

20. Which of the following issue(s) do you think is the biggest challenge in China-US relations? (You can choose more than one.)
    (a) Trade disputes
    (b) Currency issues
    (c) Taiwan issue
    (d) Human rights issues
    (e) Cybersecurity
    (f) Democratic politics
    (g) Energy and environmental issues
    (h) Diaoyu/Senkaku Islands dispute
    (i) South China Sea disputes
    (j) Other questions (please list) --------

(continued)

(continued)

21. 您认为哪个国家对中国的国家安全的威胁最大?

(a) 澳大利亚
(b) 朝鲜
(c) 俄罗斯
(d) 菲律宾
(e) 美国
(f) 日本
(g) 印度
(h) 英国
(i) 越南
(j) 其他国家 (请注明)

21. Which one of the following countries do you think poses the greatest threat to China's national security?

(a) Australia
(b) North Korea
(c) Russia
(d) Philippines
(e) United States
(f) Japan
(g) India
(h) United Kingdom
(i) Vietnam
(j) Other countries (please specify)

22. 您认为在下述哪些问题上中国和美国拥有共同的利益? (您可以有多个选择)

(a) 贸易
(b) 核不扩散(伊朗和朝鲜)

(c) 台湾
(d) 能源
(e) 人权
(f) 网络安全
(g) 金融稳定
(h) 反恐
(i) 气候变化
(j) 其他(请列举)---

22. In which of the following issues do you think China and the United States share common interests? (You can choose more than one.)

(a) Trade
(b) Nuclear non-proliferation (Iran and North Korea)
(c) Taiwan
(d) Energy
(e) Human rights
(f) Cybersecurity
(g) Financial stability
(h) Counter-terrorism
(i) Climate change
(j) Others (please list) ---

23. 有人说中国外交在2008-9世界金融危机后变的更强硬了,您的看法是:
(a) 完全同意
(b) 有保留地同意
(c) 有点不同意
(d) 完全不同意
(e) 不清楚

23. Some say that China's foreign policy has become more assertive after the 2008-9 global financial crisis. Do you agree?
(a) Agree
(b) Agree with reservation
(c) Somewhat disagree
(d) Completely disagree
(e) Not clear

24. 您如何评价中国与东盟的关系?

(a) 非常好
(b) 一般好
(c) 不好不坏(非敌非友)
(d) 敌对关系
(e) 不清楚

24. How would you describe China–ASEAN relations now?

(a) Very good
(b) Good
(c) Neither good nor bad
(d) Antagonistic
(e) Not clear

(*continued*)

(continued)

25. 如果中国和日本在钓鱼岛发生武装冲突, 您认为美国会武装介入吗?
    (a) 非常可能
    (b) 有可能
    (c) 不太可能
    (d) 根本不可能
    (e) 不清楚

25. If there is an armed conflict between China and Japan over the Diaoyu/Senkaku Islands, do you think the United States would intervene?
    (a) Very likely
    (b) Likely
    (c) Unlikely
    (d) Very unlikely
    (e) Not clear

26. 您如何评价目前中国和俄罗斯的关系?
    (a) 非常好
    (b) 一般好
    (c) 不好不坏(非敌非友)
    (d) 敌对关系
    (e) 不清楚

26. How would you describe China–Russia relations now?
    (a) Very good
    (b) Good
    (c) Neither good nor bad
    (d) Antagonistic
    (e) Not clear

27. 您如何评价目前中国和非洲的关系?
    (a) 非常好
    (b) 一般好
    (c) 不好不坏(非敌非友)
    (d) 敌对关系
    (e) 不清楚

27. How would you describe China–Africa relations now?
    (a) Very good
    (b) Good
    (c) Neither good nor bad
    (d) Antagonistic
    (e) Not clear

28. 您如何评价目前中国和拉丁美洲的关系?
    (a) 非常好
    (b) 一般好
    (c) 不好不坏(非敌非友)
    (d) 敌对关系
    (e) 不清楚

28. How would you describe China–Latin America relations now?
    (a) Very good
    (b) Good
    (c) Neither good nor bad
    (d) Antagonistic
    (e) Not clear

29. 您如何评价目前中国和印度的总体关系?
    (a) 非常好
    (b) 一般好
    (c) 不好不坏(非敌非友)
    (d) 敌对关系
    (e) 不清楚

29. How would you describe China–India relations now?
    (a) Very good
    (b) Good
    (c) Neither good nor bad
    (d) Antagonistic
    (e) Not clear

30. 您如何评价中国和日本之间总体关系?
    (a) 非常好
    (b) 一般好
    (c) 不好不坏(非敌非友)
    (d) 敌对关系
    (e) 不清楚

30. How would you describe China–Japan relations now?
    (a) Very good
    (b) Good
    (c) Neither good nor bad
    (d) Antagonistic
    (e) Not clear

(*continued*)

(continued)

31. 有人认为恢复六方会谈是解决朝鲜问题的关键, 您如何评价?

   (a) 非常同意
   (b) 有保留地同意
   (c) 有点不同意
   (d) 完全不同意
   (e) 不清楚

32. 您认为中国是现有国际秩序的挑战者吗?
   (a) 非常同意
   (b) 同意
   (c) 有点不同意
   (d) 完全不同意
   (e) 不清楚

33. 您如何评价中国整体的外交政策?
   (a) 很强硬
   (b) 强硬但有度
   (c) 有点软弱
   (d) 很软弱
   (e) 不清楚

34. 有人说, 中国应该与其他国家缔结军事同盟或发展军事同盟性质的"伙伴关系", 您的态度是:
   (a) 非常同意
   (b) 同意但有保留
   (c) 有点不同意
   (d) 完全不同意
   (e) 不清楚\

35. 您是否认为中国应该改变对朝鲜的政策?
   (a) 非常同意
   (b) 同意但有保留
   (c) 有点不同意
   (d) 完全不同意
   (e) 不清楚

36. 您如何评价中国和欧盟之间的关系?
   (a) 非常好
   (b) 一般好
   (c) 不好不坏(非敌非友)
   (d) 敌对关系
   (e) 不清楚

31. Some people believe that the Six-Party Talks are central to resolving the North Korean nuclear crisis. Do you agree?
   (a) Agree
   (b) Agree with reservation
   (c) Somewhat disagree
   (d) Completely disagree
   (e) Not clear

32. Do you think China is a challenger to the existing world order?
   (a) Strongly agree
   (b) Somewhat agree
   (c) Somewhat disagree
   (d) Strongly disagree
   (e) Not clear

33. How would you evaluate China's overall foreign policy?
   (a) Very strong
   (b) Strong with restraint
   (c) Weak
   (d) Very weak
   (e) Not clear

34. It has been said that China should build military alliances or partnerships with other countries. Do you agree?

   (a) Strongly agree
   (b) Agree with reservations
   (c) Somewhat disagree
   (d) Completely disagree
   (e) Not clear

35. Do you think China should change its policy toward North Korea?
   (a) Strongly agree
   (b) Agree with reservations
   (c) Somewhat disagree
   (d) Completely disagree
   (e) Not clear

36. How would you describe China–EU relations now?
   (a) Very good
   (b) Good
   (c) Neither good nor bad
   (d) Antagonistic
   (e) Not clear

(*continued*)

(continued)

37. 中国应该改变韬光养晦的外交政策吗?	37. Should China change its foreign policy principle of *Taoguang Yanghui*?
(a) 非常同意	(a) Strongly agree
(b) 同意但有保留	(b) Agree with reservations
(c) 有点不同意	(c) Somewhat disagree
(d) 完全不同意	(d) Completely disagree
(e) 不清楚	(e) Not clear

Note: Some questions are not asked in all four years. Please refer to the chapters for more detail

Index[1]

[1] Note: Page numbers followed by 'n' refer to notes.

© The Author(s) 2019
H. Feng et al., *How China Sees the World*,
https://doi.org/10.1007/978-981-15-0482-2

China (*cont.*)
  censorship, 8
  as challenger, 12
  and climate change, 37, 63, 110
  constitutional reform, 8
  "consultative involvement"
      approach, 90
  diplomacy, 111
  foreign policy behaviour, 1, 92
  government, 1–4, 7, 9, 21, 22,
      27–29, 31, 33, 50, 57, 59, 76,
      78–80, 90, 94, 104, 105
  hard power, 27–32
  humanitarian interventions, 90
  and India, 4, 10, 13, 78, 82, 83, 86,
      92, 94
  international order, 12, 21–40, 108
  "keeping-a-low-profile" (TGYH
      principle), 13, 71, 103
  leaders (*see* Chinese leaders)
  "Made in China 2025" policy,
      28, 109
  major power diplomacy, 71
  market-oriented reforms, 109
  middle class, 6
  multilateral diplomacy, 83
  nationalism, 25, 109
  "new type of major power relations"
      (NTMPR), 63, 64
  non-alliance policy, 10, 71, 74,
      78, 89
  "non-interference" policy, 89
  and North Korea, 54, 71, 76–78,
      90, 94, 102, 105, 106
  policy makers, 3, 8, 14, 22, 45, 61,
      65, 94, 101–103
  policy outcomes, 1
  power, 12, 21–40, 47, 108
  power capabilities, 7, 12, 22–39
  public opinion, 2–7, 14, 15n6
  public opinion research, 3–7
  relations with US, 10, 40, 60, 103
      (*see also* US–China relations)

as rising Asian hegemon, 24
as rising superpower, 24, 25
and Russia, 78, 89, 91, 103
scholars (*see* International relations
    scholars (China))
soft power, 27–32
striving for achievement (YSZW
    principle), 88, 89
China Foreign Affairs University, 12,
    70n44
China Institute of Contemporary
    International Relations, 12
China Institute of International
    Studies, 12
China Strategic Culture Promotion
    Association, 9
Chinese Academy of Social
    Sciences, 4, 12
Chinese Century, 89
Chinese Community of Political
    Science and International
    Studies (CCPSIS), 2, 22, 46,
    72, 102
Chinese IR scholars, *see* International
    relations scholars (China)
Chinese leaders
    attitudes, 2
    perceptions, 2, 22
Churchill, W., 6
Climate change, 37, 54, 56, 57, 62,
    63, 110
Clinton, B., 3
Cold War, 8, 23, 60, 65
Cooperation, 5, 13, 57, 59, 61–63,
    79, 83, 89, 91–93, 103, 110, 111
Cyber security, 49, 51, 54

D
Davos World Economic Forum, 102
Democracy
    pluralist theory, 6
    as US–China issue, 50